# BASEBALL
## TECHNIQUES IN
# PICTURES

## Michael Brown

Book Consultant:

## Tom Kuncl

Assistant Baseball Coach at the
University of North Carolina

A Perigee Book

Perigee Books are published by
The Putnam Publishing Group
200 Madison Avenue
New York, NY  10016

Library of Congress Cataloging-in-Publication Data

Brown, Michael.
    Baseball techniques in pictures / Michael Brown.
    Book consultant, Tom Kuncl.
        p.        cm.
    "A Perigee book"
    ISBN  0-399-51798-7
    I.Baseball. II. Brown, Michael. III. Kuncl, Tom. IV. Title.
GV867.876  1993        92-44226 CIP
796.357—dc20

Cover design by Lisa Amoroso

Front cover photograph © by
Brian Drake/SportsChrome East-West

Printed in the United States of America
            6 7 8 9 10

This book is printed on acid-free paper.

∞

# Table of Contents

# Introduction

Baseball is special. Players of any age can have lots of fun and get great exercise playing many team sports; however, you will find, when you practice hard and play to win, that baseball offers unique challenges and rewards. Pitching, hitting, and fielding are complex skills—even the pros must continually practice and hone these skills. And, of course, baseball is special because it is the quintessential American sport. Baseball is as symbolic of the United States as the fifty stars of our flag, and at the same time has been embraced and excelled at by many different nations around the world. From China to Cuba, from the outskirts of Tokyo to the fields of the Philippines and Venezuela, the whole world knows that baseball has something special to offer.

This book is designed to help players who are just starting to become familiar with the baseball skills and techniques that are second nature to successful ball players and coaches. It's written in direct, easy-to-understand language and provides coaches simple descriptions of specific techniques. We hope you find this guide to the unique skills of baseball useful.

Beyond general fitness, you don't have to be especially tall or strong to succeed at baseball—but few sports require more intelligence, quickness, coordination, and savvy. Especially at the beginning level, heart and smarts are your most important qualities. Remember two things: First, *everyone* from you to George Brett began as a young and inexperienced player; second, baseball is a team sport—you and your teammates are in it together. It helps to have a brilliant catcher, a star pitcher, and a knock-'em-outta-the-park hitter on your side, but it is a team's collective skill that brings victory. Be dedicated, work hard, and never forget to have fun.

The techniques that make up good batting, pitching, and catching are discussed step by step from starting stance to completion of the action. We emphasize those techniques that are used by individual players, and for the most part leave strategy to the team manager. For instance, we describe and illustrate how to catch fly balls, develop a powerful overhand throw, and take a proper batting stance, as well as some good techniques for bunting and stealing bases. The manager, however, is the best one to tell young players *when* to bunt, steal a base, or walk a batter.

We also cover equipment and clothes—their proper fit and use—in the appropriate place. For instance, before the catcher's technique is covered in the last half of Part Two, the catcher's equipment is covered in detail, along with some tips and precautions about wearing it.

## PRACTICE

To become a good player, it's important to work hard to perfect your skills and techniques during practice. In an actual game, under pressure, it can be much more difficult to perform. Only through practice will good techniques become instincts that emerge during the game. When you walk out on the practice diamond, you must be mentally and physically ready to practice good habits and support your teammates. Then you must work to understand the strategy and tactics of the game so you can call on the appropriate skills at the right time.

Of course, playing baseball is more fun than practicing, and winning is more fun than losing. To win you must compete and be aggressive, but the most important and productive kind of competition will always be with yourself, striving always to improve your skills. Cal Ripkin got to be a superstar only by striving to perform every action, even the smallest, as perfectly as possible, and always admitting that there was room for improvement. If you do this, set reasonable goals, and keep them foremost in your mind—not winning and losing, but improving, excelling, and having fun—you can't lose.

One particular stumbling block to look out for: don't get so hung up on playing a certain position that you make yourself miserable when you don't get to play there. Instead, try to honestly ask yourself, "What position is right for me?" Physical type won't matter as much in baseball as in some other sports—but size, skill level, and whether you are right- or left-handed may influence what position you play.

Without letting that lock you in, use it to your advantage to be both a better player and a better team member. As the seasons progress, experiment with your coach to find the places that use your talents and give you the most satisfaction. Even when you make a position yours, learning baseball well requires that on top of knowing your position intimately, you must have general knowledge and an overall ability to perform in any position. Sometimes a teammate can't make it and you will be called on to fill in. This will be your chance to show what you have learned. Work on building up skill, strength, and increasing your ball smarts. By striving to strengthen your body, improve coordination, and speed up reaction time, you can transform yourself into an athlete.

Again, we hope the time you spend practicing the techniques in this book gives you an advantage on the field and helps you to excel in and enjoy the game.

## SAFETY

Now, before we get to the specific skills and techniques that make up baseball, a few words about safety.

You don't have to get hit by a bat or ball to be injured—pulled muscles and worse can occur when you don't warm up before practice or play. Warming up and warming down is essential in order to get your muscles limbered up and ready for play.

When practicing with your team, a coach should have everyone warm up, but you also should warm up if you're alone or just hitting fungoes with some friends. Start with a slowish jog around the field, followed by a few gentle jumping jacks to get your blood flowing. Next, do some stretches. Don't bounce during your stretching exercises, but stretch slowly and deliberately, controlling your muscles. Here are some examples:

*Trunk twisters.* Stand with your feet apart about as far as your shoulders. Bend your arms and raise them shoulder level, parallel to the ground, pointing your elbows straight out, then twist your upper torso back and forth to stretch your back and hips.

*Toe touching.* Stand with your feet together, then slowly bend and touch your feet, with your legs straight. Then bend your knees slightly and slowly rise.

*Hammerlock.* This will stretch your shoulders and back. Stand with your feet spread slightly, raise one arm straight up, then with your other hand push the elbow back *gently* until your forearm rests on the back of your head. Alternate arms.

*Hurdler's stretch.* Standing, bend at the waist. Put one leg forward, with only the heel touching the ground. Holding the forward leg straight, stretch down and touch the toes with both hands. Repeat with the other leg.

Warming down is also important; it will help reduce soreness after a tough workout. If you usually walk fifteen blocks home after a session on the field, that should do it. But if you're going to step from vigorous exercise on the field into a twenty-minute car ride, save time for a brisk walk around the field and a few stretches, or you'll be very sore next morning and probably pretty clumsy at your next practice. To warm down your throwing arm, you and a friend could continue with a few gentle throws. Or, you could continue making throwing motions—the important thing is to not abruptly stop the arm motion.

The right shoes and clothing is another safety issue. Cleats *are* best for baseball. Sure, you can play in an old pair of tennis shoes, but they won't offer the same kind of traction that good cleats will. Metal spikes aren't allowed in some leagues, so it's probably best to get rubber or plastic cleats instead. Be wary of using hand-me-downs—worn-out or ill-fitting cleats won't do you any favors.

Also, make sure your cleats fit. Ill-fitting shoes will affect your performance and could hurt your feet. With shoes that fit well, your weight will be evenly distributed over the cleats. Check your shoes from time to time to make sure they're wearing evenly. If a few cleats are wearing down more than all the others, your shoes might not fit properly and might be unstable. Bad running form also might cause the cleats to wear unevenly. If the upper droops over the sole, the shoes are too narrow for your foot.

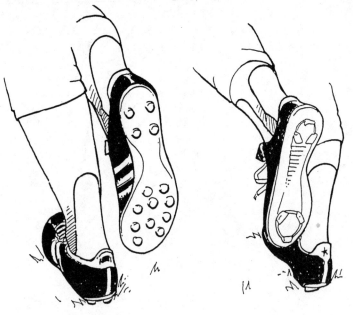

As for uniforms, they not only look great, they protect. Even if your team or league's uniforms are only numbered, same-color t-shirts, you should always wear long pants, not shorts, to prevent cuts and scrapes. Also, in the dugout when it's cool, wear a jacket to insulate your warmed-up body. Pitchers should always wear a jacket off the field. Watch TV and see how the major league pitchers never go without a jacket. And, gentlemen, a jockstrap with a cup is a very good idea too.

Later, in the appropriate sections, we offer some broad guidelines for fitting gloves and masks and choosing bats. Be mindful of the importance of your equipment—slick shoes and ill-fitting gear can be unsafe.

Finally, it's hot nearly everywhere in the United States in July and August, prime baseball time. Wear sunscreen and a cap. Beware of the combination of too much heat and too little fluid; it can lead to heat exhaustion and heatstroke. Drink plenty of fluids at practice during water breaks, whether you feel thirsty or not. If you do feel like the heat's getting to you, take a break in the shade. Heatstroke can be fatal.

# 1. Defense

Even for someone who's been dragged to the ball park against their will, a home run is exciting, but players and coaches know that defense is where most games are won or lost. Defense uses the vast majority of the skills and techniques of the game, and if you know what you're doing on defense, you can consistently help your team succeed. This means that you, the individual player, must practice and perfect your skills so you can play good solid defense every time you step on the field. You'll have hitting slumps—weeks may go by without a base hit—but if a team neglects defense, something they can play well *every day*, they will never be big winners, no matter how many hot hitters they have on the team.

Whether you play the infield or the outfield, pitcher or catcher, you must master all the basic skills of defense and practice doing them *correctly*, over and over. It is the repetition of the *correct* motions that turns them into instincts.

# Catching

## YOUR GLOVE

Like hands, gloves come in all sizes. Making a good match between your hand and a glove is important. A glove that swallows your hand isn't any good. At the other extreme, younger players may already have outgrown the glove they used last year, and the one that was used by three older brothers may not be "good and broken in," but worn out.

In a well-fitting glove, the heel of your hand should protrude slightly from the glove and the finger openings should enclose your fingers and be snug, but not tight. Ask your coach for help. You won't be able to handle the ball well with a glove that fits your hand poorly!

An infielder's glove is usually a different size from the outfielder's. The infielder uses a smaller one, the outfielder the largest they can manage. The reason infielders use smaller gloves is that seconds matter when they are trying to throw opponents out. In the extra bit of time it takes to get hold of the

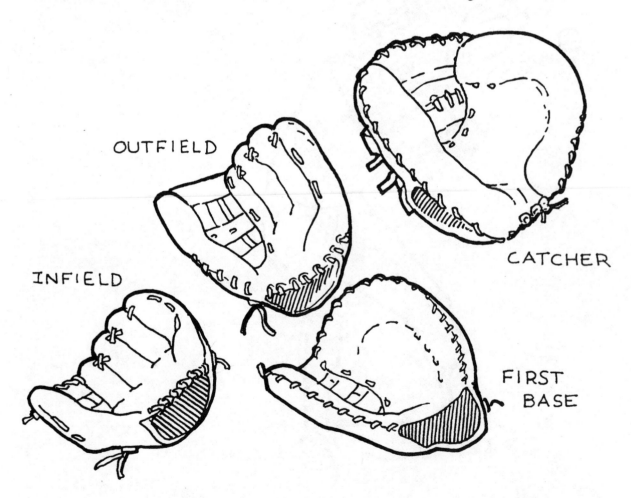

OUTFIELD

CATCHER

INFIELD

FIRST
BASE

ball and pull it from a large glove, a runner might make it to the next base. Get the right size glove for you and your position.

When you get a new glove, you need to break it in. Soak the entire glove in warm water for ten minutes. Then remove it from the water, tie a ball into it overnight, and the next day oil it. This process should cause a large round receptive pouch to form.

After you have begun to form a pocket, concentrate on breaking the glove down by bending the fingers forward into the palm. Don't break the glove across by pressing the thumb to the pinkie, because this will cause the glove to lose its shape. It will not form the right shape for fielding ground balls and it will tend to close when it's at rest—which means you'll have to open it up to catch the ball. Saddle soap, glove oil, or leather oil will also help make your glove supple.

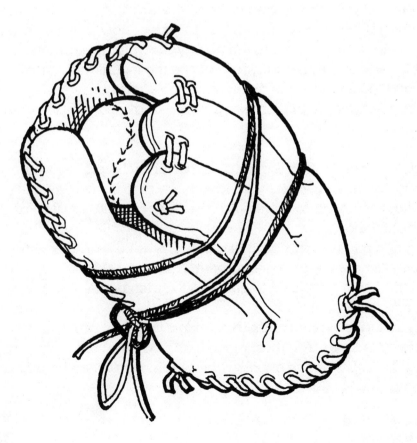

## FIELDING

Reacting to the ball, catching, and throwing it where it needs to go is called fielding. To be any help to your team, whether you're playing at first base or in left field, you must learn to catch and then you must learn to throw: the basics of fielding.

In developing good fielding habits, the number-one rule is to *keep the ball in front of you*. Whether you're backing up to keep the ball from dropping behind you, moving sideways in the infield, or moving toward the ball, keeping the ball in front of you should be your main goal.

Another very important rule of fielding is to keep watching the ball all the way into your glove. With things like gusts of wind and spin to consider (with fly balls) and the condition of the field (with grounders), you can never assume anything until you've fielded the ball.

Some parts of fielding are relatively easy to master, while others are much more difficult. For instance, the skills of moving quickly to the ball and throwing hard don't come easily—a lot of practice is required. One good way to work on throwing skill is for two players to begin throwing the ball over a short distance and gradually increase the distance. Many hours of this will improve anyone's throwing ability. Combining a long run to the ball with a *clean* catch and a strong, accurate throw takes even more work. Developing competitive skills will always demand long and hard practice before you feel confident and perform better. Be patient—if you work hard, you can do it.

Good fielding demands that you catch line drives, wild throws, ground balls, pop-up flies, and high arcing balls on the warning track. There's no simple formula, but here are some working ideas of how to perform certain techniques. Once you grasp them, it's up to you to practice, practice, practice. It is very important that you practice the technique *correctly*. Practicing bad technique is like memorizing the wrong answers for a test. When you're spending all that time at practice, *make sure you're doing it right*.

Learning the ingredients of a good clean catch is the place to start. Without being able to catch, you won't even have the ball to throw. Resist the temptation to rush ahead to something more exciting—basics first, and the first basic is catching.

The first time you put on a baseball glove, it was new and exciting. Gradually, wearing it began to feel normal and natural. Just as you had to get used to the glove, you need to get used to catching the ball properly so that good form feels natural.

Catching includes *moving to the ball*, *extending your arms*, and *bending*. It uses your whole body. You must move to the ball and use *both* your hands. No matter if the ball is above or below the waist, always use both hands for catching balls.

Before ball meets glove, you must get your body ready. Here's how to prepare:

1. Get ready—the defensive stance.
2. Determine the direction of the ball.
3. Move toward the ball.

## THE DEFENSIVE STANCE

In any sport, players get into a ready position when anticipating periods of intense action. Players hold themselves in a particular "get set" stance as they await the action, and then shift into the ready stance when the action begins.

*Get set.* For the set position, stand with your feet a bit farther apart than your shoulders to give you solid support. Turn your toes out a bit to make side-to-side or lateral moves easier. Then bend your knees and lower your body: more if you're in the infield, less in the outfield, because outfielders often will have to straighten up and sprint.

Hold your throwing-side foot back a bit, making it easier for you to push off on your bare-hand side. Poise with your weight more on the balls of your feet than your heels. Hold your glove open and hands relaxed about knee height (higher for outfielders). With your back straight and your head up, stay alert for the actions of the pitcher, catcher, batter, and runners. Think with your body as you watch the action and see and sense what is coming.

*Get ready.* When the pitcher throws, get ready. You now alter your position slightly. Transfer your weight more to the balls of your feet—if this seems too awkward, you were too far forward before. Your heels should be slightly off the ground and you should bend your knees a bit more. Keep your back straight and head up, but raise your hands slightly and keep your eyes on the ball. You are poised and ready to burst into action in whatever direction you're needed. It might help to go ahead and take a few stutter steps so you won't be frozen when the ball is hit. Remember, outfielders start out less crouched and end up much more erect in the ready position.

Just tossing mixed grounders and pop-ups with a friend is a good opportunity to practice the set/ready positions. However you do it, you should practice until it feels natural and you just naturally move into the stance when the pitcher winds up.

## DETERMINE THE DIRECTION OF THE BALL

Once you've learned the ready position, you must learn to judge the ball's motion and predict where it's going.

First, be intently watching for the contact between bat and ball. You must have your eyes on the right spot at the right instant to begin following the ball's motion. Teach yourself to watch and judge the flight of the ball as soon as it is hit, and to move where the ball can be played as soon as the judgment is made. This is the only way you're going to be able to reach the ball in time. At the very beginning of your baseball career, you might have trouble with this, but with much practice and play, you'll develop an instinct for it.

## MOVE TO THE BALL

A ball will very rarely come right to you. Oftentimes in the big-league games on TV, it seems like the ball drops right in a player's glove, but, in truth, he got there and got in front of the ball before the camera had time to find it.

When you think you know where the ball's headed, the next step is to get your body in front of the ball. Remember, first and foremost, strive to *keep the ball in front of you.* Move to the ball, backwards or laterally, and place yourself so you can *squarely face* the ball as it comes to you.

There are a couple of ways to back up. Over shorter distances, simply step backwards. If you have more ground to cover, turn around and run with your back to the ball, looking over your shoulder. The advantage of backpedaling is that you never have to take your eyes off the ball and you are already facing the ball to catch it. When you must move faster, however, it's better to turn around and run. It's harder to keep your eye on the ball, so be sure to turn back around as quickly as you can when you reach the spot where it will drop.

When moving side to side, you can use a simple side step, shuffling the feet, but not crossing them. This is good for short distances. If you must quickly travel a fairly good distance, use a crossover step to get yourself turned in that direction and run face forward. This can be fast and effective, but also tricky. Don't get tangled! Infielders use the crossover step when they must reach a ball some distance away. You must *snap* into the crossover step and make this first step a big one, but comfortable enough so you can drive forward from that big step without losing your balance. Turn your upper body in the same direction, while pivoting on the ball of the foot nearest the ball.

Now, keeping your strides low, run to the spot where you hope to intersect the ball. A slight banana curve back may help you get behind the ball. Infielders should keep their gloves down as they move toward the ball. Don't lazily stride to the side of the ball, then poke your arm out to reach it. Move and get in front of the ball!

## GENERAL PRINCIPLES OF CATCHING

*Extend your arms.* Before the ball arrives, extend your arms toward it. Resist the impulse to extend an arm out to the side for the ball. Extending your arms is good—but do it out in front of your body, with elbows and wrists relaxed, so you don't catch the ball up against your body. With your arms extended, you'll get the ball sooner. Now, as the ball hits your glove, relax your arms to cushion its impact. Your whole body should remain slightly flexed, and be sure not to lock up your knees.

*Use both hands.* It's important to catch the ball in the pocket of the glove, not with the fingers. Use the fingers to control the ball, the pocket to hold it. Whether you catch it above or below the waist, always remember to catch *with both hands.* While the glove will take most of the impact, your ungloved hand is also a key partner in capturing the ball.

When catching, your two hands should come together like the jaws of a Venus' flytrap. Catch the ball in the glove pocket and trap it with the other hand. If you catch and hold the ball properly with your hands as soon as you catch it, and don't press it against your ribs, you'll be able to throw the ball that much more quickly.

A good exercise for several players is to get a couple of old pot lids and try catching the ball with one of them. By holding the lid in your glove hand, you are forced to use both hands!

*Catching above and below the waist.* Balls above the waist should be caught with the fingers pointing upward, thumbs together, and hands forming a W. Below-the-waist balls should be caught with the fingers pointing down, little fingers together, forming an M.

This is just about the only way to consistently use both hands on catches. It's a good rule, because it makes two-handed catches seem easier and makes them more controllable.

## FIELDING A GROUNDER

In the infield, a ground ball can come at you very fast. You must move quickly, and your most important goal is to *stop the ball from getting beyond the infield!*

In the ready position, with your glove hanging down and in front of your body, watch the ball as it enters the hitting zone. Be ready to get in front of the ball and stop it. Catching it is best, of course, but if you can't do that, your body must back up your hands so the ball will hit you and drop in front of you.

Outfielders should remember that they will almost always charge up to a grounder, and very rarely back up for it. Charging to the ball gets you to it faster and therefore helps you throw runners out. Especially with slower balls, if you stand there and wait for the ball to reach you, the runners may already have reached the next base.

When fielding a grounder, bending at the knees lessens the chances of the ball going under your glove. Some players drop to one knee, but they lose a little time standing back up for the throw. A one-handed standing stab at a grounder is sometimes necessary, especially for infielders. But if you try this on a routine grounder and flub it, it could mean a two- or three-base error. Don't do it unless you must.

Carefully watch the way the ball is hopping or bouncing. When it's taking a lot of small hops, capture it close to the ground with your glove fingers pointing down, palm up, and your throwing hand ready to steady it into the glove as it hits.

When a ball is taking big bounces, run toward it and try to get it at the top of a bounce, with your glove fingers up.

Remember, catch balls above the waist with your thumbs together and hands making a W. For balls lower than your belt, crouching is best. And remember, here your fingers will be together, forming an M.

*Do not* step to the side of the ball's path and try to snap it with your glove. You are far more likely to miss it this way, and if do miss it, it's gone. If you miss the ball when you're in front of it, at least your body will stop it.

## CATCHING FLY BALLS

Judging a fly ball becomes easier with practice and experience. In time, you will be able to judge fairly well where the ball will land as soon as it is hit. And, if you move to that place fast enough, you'll even have time to compensate for wind, ball spin, or misjudgment.

Generally, players shift positions on the field according to the hitters' strengths, weaknesses, and what kind of balls they tend to hit. Whether they are right- or left-handed hitters comes next as a consideration. When a left-handed hitter steps up to the plate, the fielders should shift toward right field and first base, since lefties tend to hit to the right of second. For a right-handed hitter, move the other way, toward left and third. This is something you and your teammates should go over during practice.

There are also tactical situations to take into account. For example, if one run will win the game for your opponents, and there is a runner on third with one out or no outs, bring in the infielders and the outfielders. The problem, of course, is that the batter may hit an easy single through the drawn-in infield or the outfielders' heads, and the runner will score and win the game. Even so, the catcher knows that the defense must stop the opposition from scoring the run at all costs.

Outfielder positioning is complicated and changes with every batter. Don't hug the fence, or you won't be able to get the short flies or get to grounders quickly enough. As you move to the ball, think about positioning yourself so you can catch the ball just above head level, elbows and wrists relaxed. Not only does this position help you catch the ball more easily, it leaves you in good position to throw quickly. You also can use your glove to shield the sun from your eyes if necessary. Your glove fingers should be up and your other hand ready to secure the ball as it hits the glove.

As always, try to get in front of the ball. In reality, for pop flies, this will mean being under the ball. Still, make sure not to let it fall behind you. For pop flies to your right or left, use the crossover step we described earlier, and remember to curve back. If you can plan it so that you take a last step or two as you catch the ball, you can continue, in fluid motion, to your throw.

# Throwing

In the long run, even great hitters hurt their teams if they can't throw accurately. Learning to throw accurately takes a good deal of effort and practice. Few players start out throwing beautifully, so every player should take time to learn, step by step, the elements of a good throw, then practice putting all the elements together. Basic throwing skills are vital for every player in every position.

Beginning players should focus on the three-quarter overhand throw. The important ingredients of competent throwing are:

- A proper grip for ball rotation
- Stance
- Raising the arm
- Shoulder rotation
- Releasing the ball
- Follow-through

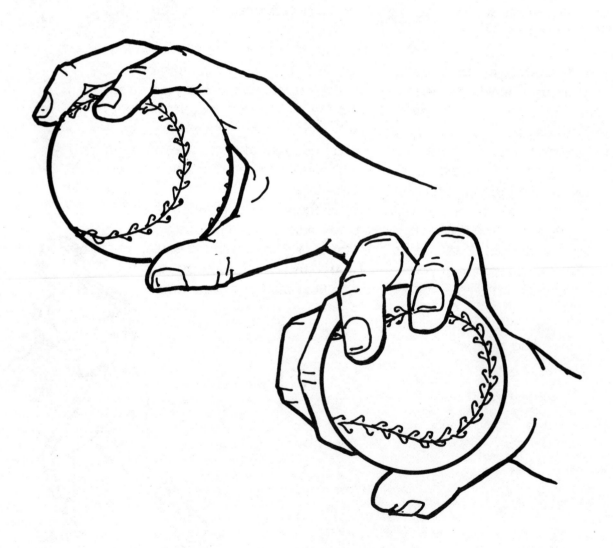

## THE GRIP

The way you hold the ball makes a great deal of difference. You get your throwing power from your arm, back, and legs, but it is your grip that gives you accuracy and control. This is not the way you'd just instinctively grab a baseball-size object. You must learn the right way to grip the ball and learn to grip it this way each time you throw.

Pitchers, of course, experiment with various kinds of grips for various pitches. No such fine tuning is necessary when you're throwing the ball. Here are the ingredients of the common baseball grip:

- Cross your middle and index fingers over the seams at the widest point, with a little less than an inch of space between them.
  The stitches give you something more to hold on to than a slick ball, and they help the ball move through the air. When you throw the ball with your fingers across the stitches, as shown in the illustration, the friction of the spinning stitches against air is even, and as a result, the passage of the ball through the air is accurate, smooth, and controllable.

- Place your thumb on the other side of the ball from the middle and index fingers, so it grips the ball with its inside edge.
  Now, with fingers and thumb placed like this, gently but firmly pinch the ball. Your thumb and index finger should form a U.

- Rest your pinkie and ring finger on the side of the ball.
  This will make your hold more secure.

- Leave a space between the ball and the palm of your hand.
  Hold the ball with your *fingers*, not your palm. Try your best to do this even if you have very small hands.

- Keep your hand *behind* the ball.
  The right grip won't matter if you swivel your wrist around and let the open side of the ball face sideways. The ball should face the direction you're going to throw it.

Once you know the proper grip, you should practice until it is the natural way you grasp the ball. You'll practice on the field, of course, but you can also practice your grip just about anywhere—on the bus on the way to school or sitting in front of the TV. The more natural it feels, and the stronger your hand, the better.

## STANCE

When you throw, you should always step in the direction of your throw with the glove-side foot. This means you'll always have your side turned toward your target. Remember to pivot with your other foot while stepping toward the target with the glove-side foot. This footwork lets you use the muscles in your shoulders and back for power. If you try a throw squarely facing your target, you'll use only your arm muscles and have no zip in the throw.

## RAISING YOUR ARM

Your throw should begin with the ball in your glove and your glove and throwing hands together somewhere between chest and waist height. Bring the ball out of the glove; first, grip the ball correctly, then raise your throwing arm *high*, with your elbow above your shoulders. Remember, as the illustration shows, your arm should be high and your elbow well above your shoulders. Your upper and lower arm form an L.

## SHOULDER ROTATION

You don't throw with your hands and arms alone. Your whole body should be involved. The more you use your larger muscles, the easier the throw will be. Shoulders should be a key part of your throw.

   After you've stepped forward, you'll be standing sideways to your target. As you throw, turn your shoulders and square them in the direction you want to throw the ball. When you first practice this movement, do it slowly. This helps teach the motion to your muscles, and then you can work on developing power.

## RELEASING THE BALL

When your hand has come up over your head and is five to eight inches past your ear, release the ball. Only trial and error can teach you the precise moment, during the movement of your arm, to release the ball. After a few hundred practice throws, you will know instinctively at what point in this fluid motion to release the ball.

You should concentrate on releasing the ball from the ends of your first and second fingers; feel the seams at your two fingertips as you let it go. Your pivot foot should come up off the ground and take a small step forward as you release the ball, helping you to maintain your balance during the follow-through.

## THE FOLLOW-THROUGH

Think of the throw as a single fluid motion that begins with the ball in the glove at your chest and ends with a follow-through after the ball is released. Good follow-through results in good control and is integrally related to the path of your throw. As your pivot foot moves forward, your body should bend forward slightly and your arm should cross all the way over and down in front of and across your chest, finishing the arc that started behind your head.

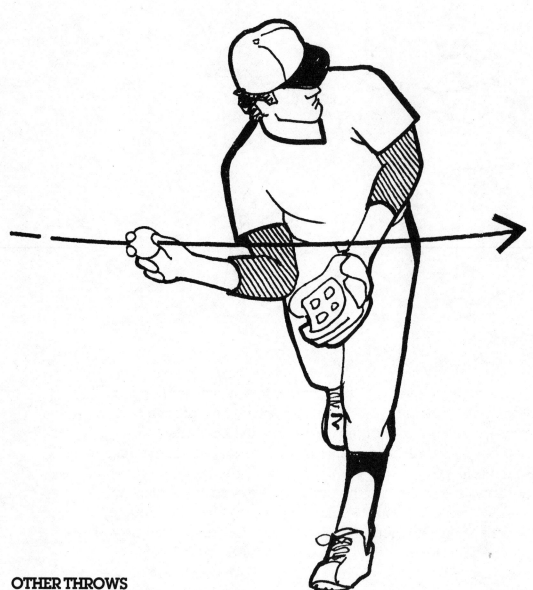

## OTHER THROWS

### Sidearm

For a sidearm throw, you release the ball at a point below your shoulders, and usually between your belt and knees if you're crouching. There are a few situations in which you must throw the ball sidearm. For example, if you're fielding a slow grounder while on the run, the runner may beat the throw if you take time to set up for the more dependable overhand throw. It's not easy to get accuracy or distance with a sidearm throw, and it puts strain on your wrist and elbow. It should be your choice only in an emergency.

If you need to throw sidearm, pick the ball up with the proper throwing grip. If you are right-handed, try to approach the ball so that as you grasp it your left foot is forward. By fielding with the left foot forward, you'll be able to throw on the very next step. Throw with your right foot coming down as you release the ball with a snap of the wrist. Clean pickup and toss is essential. Also remember that a sidearm toss will tend to veer in the direction of the spin.

## Underhand Toss

You use the underhand toss only when you are close to the receiving player. You do it to save time when you field a ball close to the ground and must release it immediately. You save time by not having to get in position, arm up, for the overhand throw. For example, if you're playing first base and you have to dive to knock down a hard-hit ball hit to your right, you underhand it to the pitcher, who will have moved over to cover first.

If you are quite close to the bag, footwork is less important. But even on a short toss you should pivot slightly toward your target. If you are fifteen or twenty feet away, you'll want to step toward the bag with your opposite foot and make sure your teammate sees the ball in your hand. Toss with stiff wrist and palm up. The ball should arrive at chest height at the top of its arc, just before your teammate reaches the base. Your follow-through consists of a few paces toward the play.

# Other Defensive Skills

While some skills are more commonly used by players in certain positions and on certain kinds of plays, *all* players should develop all-around baseball skills and have the ability to do everything described here.

## BARE HANDED PICK UP AND THROW

Sometimes the ball will have stopped or nearly stopped by the time it reaches you. In this case, field the ball with your bare hand and immediately throw it. In fact, you can develop the ability to field it and throw it all in one motion. Usually you'll use a sidearm for this, but remember, this is not for slow grounders, only for balls that are completely still or just barely moving. Major leaguers sometimes barehand even slow grounders—to get a fast runner, for instance. It can save precious seconds when you don't have time to catch with both hands, transfer the ball to the throwing hand, then position yourself and throw the usual three-quarter overhand. Instead, you can just scoop and toss.

Right-handers should bend at the knees, chest over the ball and right foot next to the ball, so they can move into the throw with their next left-foot step. Try to scoop slightly under the ball rather than pluck it from the top. Remember—slow-hit grounders should be fielded with your glove. To field them barehanded is just showing off.

## DIVING

At times a batted ball is traveling so fast or so far out of reach that you know you can't get in front of it, much less catch it with both hands. In order to stop it in the infield, you must *dive*.

Sometimes, the dive pays off so well that you don't just prevent an extra-base hit, you actually retire a runner. Dives will never feel good, but with your team cheering you can stand it. You will find that diving doesn't hurt as much as you imagine, and here are a few steps to help you make that great leap and avoid injury.

Practice diving, first from your knees, then standing, then from the ready position, and finally from a crossover step. Keep your bare hand up and out of the way. Don't use this hand to break your fall—you might break *it*.

If you dive for the ball and stop it, but don't catch it, get up on your knees or feet as fast as you can, field it with your bare hand, and throw it.

## DOUBLE PLAY

When playing defense, there's nothing more exciting than pulling off a successful double play. Of course, the most common double play is a force-out at second base and then a throw to first for the second out. This is the most common type because one of the most common situations in baseball is a runner on first and no runners on any other bases. When the ball is hit in this situation, the runner on first is, of course, forced to move to second. In addition, the fielders have no other runners to concern themselves with and they're not trying to stop a runner in scoring position from advancing. The second baseman, shortstop, and first baseman are usually the players involved. However, double plays are certainly not limited to this situation. Any fielder may be in on a double play and should look for opportunities to create them.

The double play has been the turning point of many games, but don't be so eager to get two outs that you don't even get one! Go for the sure out. Remember, when attempting to turn a double play, *always make sure of the first out.*

For example, don't get in such a rush that you make a wild throw to second and allow *both* runners extra bases. Or, if you're playing second base, concentrate first on a good catch and dragging your foot over the base. Keeping too close a track on the hitter, who's moving to first, or the runner sliding into second could cause you to fumble your catch. Throws should be at chest height, and remember: not every play can be a double play.

## THE PIVOT PLAYER

In a typical double play, the player who catches the ball and tags second base, then turns and tries to throw the hitter out, is called the "pivot." When you field the ball, don't make the pivot work any harder than necessary. Make sure he can see the ball. Especially when you're quite close to second base, pull the ball from your glove—show him the ball—and throw it; time your throw to arrive before the onrushing pivot player does. The pivot player needs an easy toss so he can concentrate on executing the necessary footwork.

If *you* are the pivot player, a quick turn and throw is essential—but make sure of that first out. Expect a poor throw and be prepared. Square your body in the direction of the throw and be ready to move to the ball. *Stay in front of the ball and catch it with both hands.*

Pay no attention to that runner barreling at you from first base. On most successful double plays, you'll have that runner forced out, the ball headed to first, and be well out of the runner's way before he arrives.

Finally, *make sure* you touch the bag.

If you're playing first base, you should always expect the throw to be bad. Of course, they won't always be bad, but be prepared. We're not encouraging you to have no faith in the second baseman, because most of them can throw well and most of them will give you good throws when they can. But a double play happens very quickly, and the runner at second is doing everything possible to disrupt the thrower. If you are always prepared for a bad throw, you'll have no problem with the good ones and a whole lot better chance of securing the haywire throws.

## DIFFERENT MOVES ON FIRST BASE

If you regularly play first base, you'll want a first-base glove. It has a much larger web for catching balls and it's built to make it easier to catch balls with the gloved hand alone. This is because you are not as compelled as other fielders to always get in front of the ball and catch it with two hands.

First basemen have one of the most continually active roles in baseball defense. Play after play, the ball comes your way. You have to balance a couple of important responsibilities: it is important that you try to stay in contact with the base so you can put the runner out—*but your first priority is to catch the ball.*

Sometimes you will have to take your foot off the base to catch the ball. Sometimes it will be necessary to stretch one arm out for the catch *while* keeping your foot on the base. Try to do both, without letting the ball get by.

As for the placement of your foot on the base, press your glove-side foot snugly against the inside edge of the bag. This will prevent the runner to first from stepping on your ankle and injuring you.

Staying on the bag won't do any good if you miss the ball. Getting the ball is more important. The stretch is important in helping you do both, but when in doubt, and especially if you have no backup, catch the ball and prevent the runners from taking extra bases.

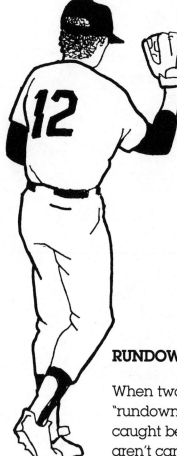

## RUNDOWNS

When two infielders trap a runner between the bases, they must execute a "rundown." If the infielders do their jobs, the runner is doomed, like a mouse caught between two cats. However, executing a rundown is tricky, and if you aren't careful he'll escape. You and your fellow infielders should:

- avoid making long throws—you might give the runner a chance to make it to a base while the ball's in the air;
- close in on the runner;
- the best strategy is to get the ball to the player *ahead* of the runner and chase him back toward the base he left;
- keep the throwing to a minimum. To do so, throw after the runner has little chance to turn around and head back toward you and away from the ball;
- when you do throw, do it to the outside or inside of the base path. A ball thrown straight along the path might hit the runner, and if so, your partner won't be able to catch the ball and the runner may make it safely;
- make sure your teammate can see the ball;
- make firm, effective throws and don't use more power than you have to—a dartlike throw is useful here;
- when you are without the ball, give your partner a clear target with your glove;
- chase the runner to the last base, not to the next one—if you make a mistake, you may give the runner a chance to advance;
- don't leave bases uncovered—you should have backup; four players should get in on the action, to cover the bases and in case of overthrows.

Beware—a runner may deliberately get into or prolong a rundown to give a teammate a chance to score from third while the defense is distracted.

## WHO CATCHES THE POP FLY?

In general, a pop-up ball should be caught by the person who is best able to run *forward* to catch it, rather than someone who must back up to it. This is no time for grandstanding. There are two reasons for calling for the ball. First, so that it won't fall unclaimed to the ground, and second, to prevent two or more players from going after it and colliding. This applies not just to pop flies, but to any ball in question. However, the situation usually occurs with pop flies.

Communication is essential. Never call pop flies too soon, and don't call the ball until it gets as high as it's going to go. Be sure to keep your eye on the ball and continue to pursue it until you either hear a teammate call for it, or are sure that the ball is yours and call it yourself.

If you call the ball too soon, it may turn out that someone else could have caught it more easily. When you are sure, yell, "Got it!" or "It's mine." (Your team should all use the same calls.)

When chasing a pop fly that is obviously going to come down near the fence or dugout, choose your spot, move there, then look for the ball. This is not a good time to keep your eyes on the ball—you may smash into the fence or pitch yourself into the dugout. Balance the need to catch the ball with protecting yourself. Extend your bare hand toward the fence as you catch, in a sensible exception to the always-two-hands rule of catching.

## HOLDING A RUNNER ON BASE

The runner has taken a lead toward the next base. The pitcher throws over to force the runner back, or maybe get the runner tagged out. That throw is called a pickoff throw. The threat of the pickoff will hold the runner on base and keep him from taking too great a lead. In a situation where there's potential for a pickoff play, take a wide stance facing the pitcher. Stay in position to take the pitcher's throw and make your tag. In the case of a pickoff at first base, your right foot should be very near the side of the bag that faces home plate. Hold your glove up for the pitcher to target.

When the pitcher makes the pickoff throw, catch and then sweep the ball in the glove down to where the runner is coming back to the bag. Whether it's a hand or foot, get your glove down quickly, tagging with the back of your glove so there's less chance the ball will be dislodged. Then quickly pull the ball back, still in your glove, ready for whatever might happen next.

## PROTECTING THIRD

Protecting third base is one situation you may have to face when playing in the infield. Let's say there's a runner on second and the batter has just hit the ball. You field a slowly hit ball or one hit to the right side of the infield. The runner on second has been taking a liberal lead and now might go for and make third.  It would be tempting to go first for the runner who's closest to scoring, but throwing out the batter is a sure thing. Go for the sure out.

If you field the ball in the left side of the infield, you have a better chance of actually making the out at third. The runner at second is looking at you to see what you'll do. Give him a convincing look while making a preliminary movement indicating that you will throw to third if he tries for it. Usually, all it will take is the right kind of look to send him back to second and you'll still have time to throw to first base for your sure out. You've got your out *and* held the runner on second.

## TAGGING A SLIDING RUNNER

Infielders need to learn how to tag a sliding runner without either player getting hurt. Don't put your feet and legs in the wrong place and don't tag in the wrong place. In general, it's best to put your feet on either side of the bag, not in front of the bag (the runner will have to knock you down) and not behind it (standing there, it will be very hard to tag him out, since the base separates you).  When the ball's caught, face the sliding runner, still with a foot on each side of the bag.

Lower the ball in the glove to the ground just in front of the bag and let the runner slide right to it. Don't reach or you'll give the runner an opportunity to slide around your tag.

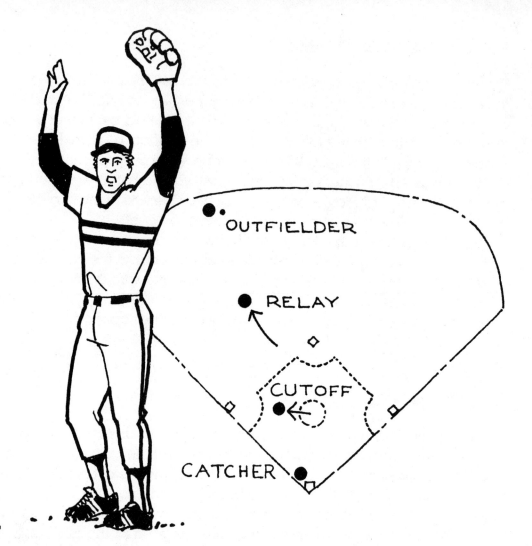

## RELAY/CUTOFF

When the ball has been driven to the fence, teamwork is essential. The hit could easily turn it into an extra-base hit or a score. The defensive priority is to get the ball to the infield in a hurry, preventing both possible scores and extra bases.

You are the outfielder. When you get hold of the ball, don't be a hero. You are facing a very long throw. To make sure you get the ball there quickly, it is usually best to relay it. You might possibly make that long throw all the way to the catcher, but it is faster and more accurate to throw the ball to a player who has stepped in between you and the ultimate target.

This relay *will* get the ball home faster. It also has another advantage: if the runner has already made it home and scored, your throw all the way home will still be hanging in the air while the batter breezes into second. But, if you've thrown to a relay or cutoff player, he'll be in a good position to change plans and throw the ball to second to prevent the hitter from advancing or to get the hitter tagged out.

Very commonly, the relay/cutoff player will be the infielder who lines up between the outfielder and the catcher on a throw to home. By positioning himself between where the ball is fielded and the catcher, the relay/cutoff is now very well lined up to receive the throw. He should raise his arms so the outfielder can quickly find him and throw. The relay throws to home if there's time, or prevents other runners from advancing.

## BACKING UP YOUR TEAMMATES

People who don't know anything about baseball have been known to watch a game for a while and feel as if "nothing happens." They are left with the impression that all baseball consists of is standing around in the field and waiting. Well, these folks are misguided. There's *always* a lot going on in good baseball. Defensive players in all positions have many responsibilities.

Along with fielding the ball and covering the bases, these players must constantly back each other up. Players in certain positions have clearly defined responsibilities to back up other specific players, and beyond that to keep their eyes open and do whatever is needed during the game. Like the order of who catches a pop fly, infield players have responsibilities for backing each other up.

Here are some examples of how these responsibilities might be carried out, depending on the game situation:

- On an extra-base hit, the pitcher might back up plays at home and at second base.
- Generally, the pitcher covers first base on sacrifice bunts or when the first baseman fields the ball.
- The shortstop might back up second or throw from right field.
- The third baseman might back up the shortstop on hard-hit balls to the left of the infield.

Your manager or coach will design a system of backups to suit your team. You should know these priorities and be there to back up your teammates. However, remember that your first responsibility is to your original area of coverage. Don't abandon your own base when a play is expected there just to back up someone else. Remember, each defensive player has a place to go on each hit ball.

# 2. The Pitcher and Catcher

## Pitching

Some people say that:

- A naturally talented athlete is the best material for making a pitcher.
- Taller pitchers throw better fastballs.

These two things are not always true. Great, maybe you have natural talent, are very tall, or both. But if neither is true about you, don't give up on pitching. Good pitchers come in all shapes and sizes.

Many youth leagues limit the number of innings that one player may pitch. No one's body, schedule, or stamina will let them throw every pitch for their team. Your team needs many good pitchers. Get working.

Okay. Don't start out thinking about breaking balls. Basics first.

Here are some realistic goals for a young pitcher:

- being able to throw strikes with your fastball
- being able to change speeds
- being able to move the ball around within the strike zone.

Before you can approach even *these* goals, you must learn some basic skills and the rudimentary mechanics of pitching. Don't forget, natural talent or not, pitching is not a naturally occurring act and it won't feel natural when you first start working on it. Also, be aware that there's more to the job of pitching than pitching. Pitchers have particular fielding responsibilities—more on that later in this chapter. First, the act of pitching.

### THE GRIP

In the section on throwing in Part One, a good basic style of grip for throwing in general was described. The pitcher's fastball grip is similar. As the illustration shows, the steps are to:

- Cross your middle finger and your index finger over the wide seams, with less than an inch of space between them.
- Place your thumb on the other side of the ball from the middle and index fingers, gripping the ball with the inside edge of your thumb. Gently and firmly pinch the ball, with your thumb and index finger forming a V.
- Rest your pinkie and ring finger on the side of the ball.

- Leave a space between the ball and the palm; hold the ball with your *fingers*, not your palm.
- Keep your hand *behind* the ball and don't swivel your wrist around and let the open side of the ball face sideways. The ball should face the direction you will throw it.

Pitchers often vary slightly this basic grip by holding the ball between the seams or on top of the long seams. This slight alteration can help you get some movement on the ball.

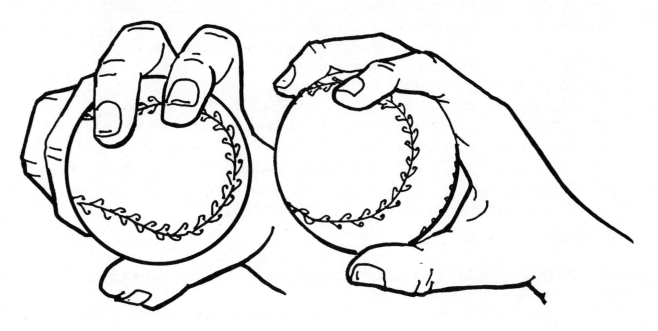

## CONTROL AND CONSISTENCY

A player—twelve years old or twenty-five—might have an arm of steel and be able to throw through the sound barrier, but he or she is no kind of pitcher without ball *control*. If you can first learn simply to throw the ball in exactly the same way two, three, and then four times, you're halfway to ball control.

Worship consistency. Develop your fastball and try to throw it the same way every single time until you can throw it in your sleep. In the beginning, everything will change slightly every time you throw. You won't ever have the same result twice. You'll change your grip, move your feet, lean back one time and sideways the next. But don't despair; instead, keep practicing. The goal of the pitcher is to be able to repeat good results. Pitching is repetitive even at the top, not just because you are a beginner. Watch the major leaguers on TV and see how each pitcher has a windup, delivery, and follow-through that varies very little from pitch to pitch. Practice is the only way to get there.

The pitch is made up of:

- Stance
- Windup
- Arm back and push off
- Arm forward and release
- Follow-through

## STANCE

The rules cover certain aspects of your pitching stance. Basically, you must always continue to touch the rubber with one foot until you release the ball. Also, you may not use your pitching stance or any motion to deceive a runner. You'll be called for a balk.

The two basic pitching stances are the *windup* and the *stretch*.

For the *windup stance*, start out facing home plate with one foot on the pitching rubber. Your other foot is free to move onto or behind the rubber. This stance gets you in a good place to make the power windup described shortly. You don't use this stance when there's a runner on first; you wouldn't be able to carry out the pickoff throw to first.

For the *stretch stance*, stand in front of the rubber with your push-off foot on the front edge of the rubber and your other foot in front of your body. This flexible stance gives you the maximum ease in throwing the pickoff while maintaining good power on your pitch.

Both the stretch and windup stances bring you to the point where you are ready to wind up.

## THE WINDUP FOR THE PITCH

This gets the momentum started. The windup is very significant, since it controls so much about what follows.

*The windup from the windup stance.* You should be facing home plate with one or both feet on the rubber. Grip the ball with your throwing hand inside the glove. You will leave your hand there right up until you start the pitch. That way, as you develop as a pitcher and begin throwing other types of pitches, you won't telegraph any information to the batter with your grip. Now:

1)  shift your body weight to your back foot;
2)  move your body weight to your forward foot; and
3)  pivot on your push-off foot and raise your striding foot, positioning your glove-side shoulder to the plate.

This windup provides a powerful pitch. Pulling your arms back and up before raising the striding foot gives the windup its power. However, it's harder to throw to a base from the windup stance, so if you're holding a runner on, the simpler stretch stance is better. You only use the windup when the bases—first and second bases, at least—are empty.

*Winding up from the stretch stance.* The *windup from the stretch* stance is an abridged version of the steps above. It eliminates the preliminary arm and backup motions and basically consists of only the final two steps of the windup.

The technique for the rest of the pitch, no matter the starting stance, is the same.

WINDUP
STANCE

STRETCH
STANCE

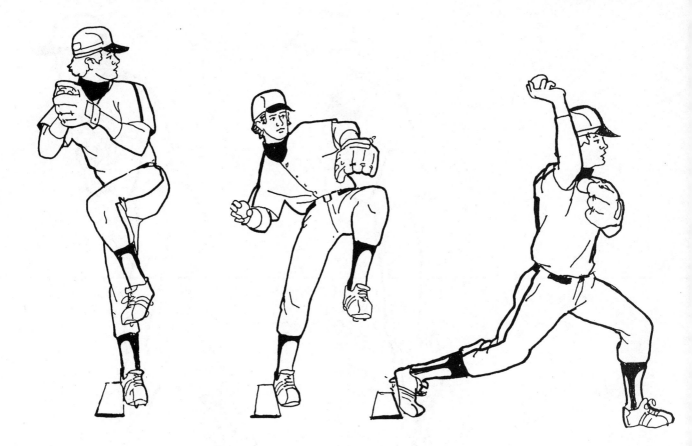

## ARM BACK AND PUSH OFF

Rock straight back away from the mound on your rear foot. *A tip for working on consistency*: with your back foot, always press on the same spot on the rubber each time. As you rock back, bring your throwing arm back. Think power: you are coiling back to put the power of your arm, body, and legs into the throw. But don't forget control.

*Avoid sidearming—bring your arm up.* Raise your elbow over your shoulder. Sometimes your arm may seem to want to swing around your side with a will of its own. It takes some practice and repetition, and it will seem that the minute you ease off, down comes that arm again. Be patient— eventually the correct way will become second nature to you.

## ARM FORWARD AND RELEASE

Channel your coiled-up energy into the release of the ball. The length of your stride as you release will greatly affect the speed and accuracy of your throw. Too short a stride, and you are not putting your leg power into the release; too long a stride gets your body too low and can cause a jerky and erratic release. It is not possible to give a certain number of inches as the best-size stride, even if everyone were exactly the same size. Finding the right stride is an individual matter.

As you stride and bring your foot down firmly and your arm around for the release, placement of your forward foot is very important. Your body and arm tend to follow the point of your foot, and so will the ball. The best placement is to have your shoe pointing straight to home. Think control.

Finally, swing your arm over your shoulder and with a snap of your wrist. Aim is important, but so is fluidity of motion. Beginning pitchers should concentrate on the strike zone and visualize the ball passing through it while feeling the ball leave their fingertips. You must be sure of your ability to consistently pitch into the strike zone before you begin to set up batters.

## FOLLOW-THROUGH

Here we describe the pitch in a series of steps, but in reality it is a single fluid motion that ends when your throwing arm passes all the way across your body.

Your best pitches will have your best, smoothest follow-through. Just as you swing *through* the ball and run *through* the base, when pitching your arm should arc all the way through the pitch. Your arm and body should stay in motion after the ball is released. Your body should move forward and down until your chest is above the front leg and your throwing arm has crossed all the way over and in front of that leg. Poor follow-through means that this path is erratic, and often means an off-target pitch.

## BASIC PITCHES

There are many pitching variations, each of which is an attempt to make the ball behave in a particular way. Pitchers don't want batters to predict their pitches. It's even better if they can lead a batter into false assumptions, then into a putout or a strikeout. All pitches are delivered with the same basic stances and moves described here, because they have to be. Just think about it. If each pitch had it's own tailored, markedly different stance and windup, you might as well flash a display like this to the batter: HERE COMES A CURVEBALL. In fact, if the batter knew it was going to curve, a curveball would be no more difficult for the batter to hit than any other ball. The strength of many pitches is the element of surprise.

What each pitch *does* have is its own grip, wrist motion, and release, which is harder for a batter to read than a stance or windup. The three basic pitches are the fastball, curveball, and off-speed or change-up. There are quite a few others, some of which have literally made the career for one major leaguer or another. However, these exotic pitches are rarely used in the lower leagues. Many coaches outlaw them altogether, for fear of ruining a developing player's fastball or his arm.

### Fastball

This is your first basic pitch to learn and the best one to use in most situations. A good fastball is intended to either sink or rise, and therefore to pass under or over the bat as it is swung. If you develop a good fastball, you will do a lot of pitching for your team, and your opponents will have a hard time hitting, much less scoring. This pitch will retire more batters than all your other pitches combined. You need strength in your arms to have a really good fastball. Daily long-throwing practice will help with that.

As the illustration shows, grip the ball across the seams. Your thumb more or less lines up with your middle finger, with the two other fingers curved along the outside of the ball. When releasing the ball from an overhand delivery, snap your wrist down just as the ball is released. When your hand passes your head, your first two fingers should be pointing at the plate. The ball should rotate rapidly backward with the long seams parallel to the ground. If you are confident of your ability to throw quite hard, this pitch is for you.

If you aren't the hardest throwing pitcher around, go for a fastball that tends to sink. For this one, grip the ball along the seams. With the same overhand release, snap your wrist down on release. With the seams rotating perpendicular to the ground, the ball will tend to sink, again misleading the batter. But be careful not to send it above the hitter's belt level, or you might deliver a very hittable ball.

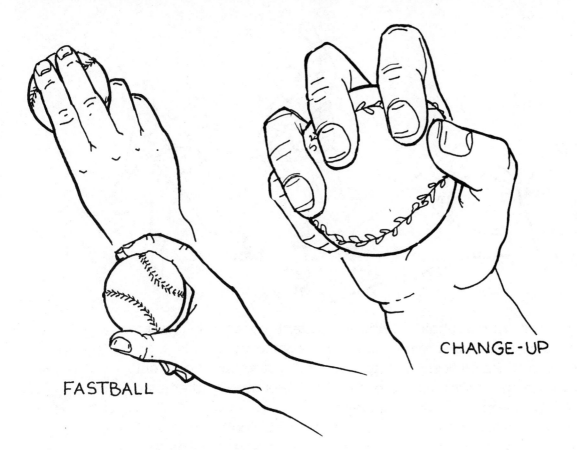

FASTBALL

CHANGE-UP

**Off-speed (also called the change-up)**

Wait till you have mastered your fastball to work on this pitch. In most respects, it's just like the fastball—only it isn't fast. The change-up pitch misleads batters and convinces them by everything you do that a fastball is coming, but it really comes more *slowly than any fastball*, making the hitter swing early. To be effective, this pitch must be thrown to a smart hitter. The hitter's got to have some ball smarts, enough to really be able to read a pitcher, and therefore to be fooled into making a prediction.

But remember, a good hitter also will be able to take a fastball right in stride; if you don't fool him and throw a simple, medium fastball, he's going to knock it to Costa Rica. However, if you throw a few good fastballs, then follow them with a change-up, your hitter will only hit thin air.

As you can see, you shouldn't practice this pitch on an opponent; don't jump the gun and try the change-up until you *know* you know how.

One commonly used grip for the change-up is to push the ball back deeper into your fingers, with your thumb alongside the ball, forming the gesture for "okay." No matter how hard you throw, the skin drag alone will slow your ball down enough to make it into a change-up.

Another grip that works is to spread three fingers across the long seams, with the ball pushed against the palm. Even with a powerful and powerful-looking overhand throw, this ball's lack of velocity will be surprising to the hitter.

But remember, since surprise is the key to the success of this pitch, always look as if you're throwing heat. It's how you release the ball, not your stance or windup, that slows the ball.

## Curveball

Fastballs dip or rise; the curveball surprises the batter by coming in closer to his hands or curving out farther to the outside of the strike zone than expected. As with a fastball or change-up, you can try a couple of different grips until you find one to stick with. The curveball is not usually attempted—much less perfected—prior to high school-level ball.

Usually, a pitcher will grip the ball as if for a sinking fastball. Again, it's the release that turns it into a curve. The other grip sometimes used is with the middle finger along one of the long seams. Either way, hold your middle and index fingers close together, with most of the throwing push coming from the middle finger. Try to get the ball going in a fast rotation toward the batter. When your arm is coming over your shoulder for the pitch, keep your hand closer to your head than you do for a fastball. Make sure to keep your elbow up. This helps with the wrist snap, which is vital to a successful curveball.

With the fastball, you snap down. But with a curve, right before the release you turn your wrist so that the ball leaves your hand over the top of your first finger and your second finger gives it spin. It spins on an angle, with all four seams spinning, slightly more downward than sideways. As with the fastball, your first two fingers will be pointing at the plate when your hand passes your head.

Normally, a right-handed pitcher will throw the curve directly "at" a right-handed batter, and it will curve out into the strike zone. The batter, judging it to be not in the strike zone, hopes for a called ball and doesn't swing. When the same pitcher throws to a lefty, the pitch appears to be going wide, seeming again not to be a strike. The batter doesn't swing—or waits too long and can't get a good one together in time. Curveballs are also thrown to make them appear to be strikes, only to drop out or inside and make the batter wave at them.

Whether it actually fools the batter or not, a good curve is just too unpredictable to give the batter enough time to swing and get a solid hit.

When you first try throwing curves, and you first get a curve going, chances are you will find it quite difficult to locate the ball. You might try practicing the curve in two stages. First, practice until you can get that curve when you try, then try for control.

## ARM CARE

Pitching is hard on your arm! If you want to go on pitching, take care of your arm.  Here are some rules to live by:

1.  When not pitching, always wear a warm-up jacket.
2.  Depend on your legs and back for pitching power. Your arm and shoulder are the tools, your legs and back the engine.
3.  Always warm up—not just your arm, but your legs and back, too.
4.  Always warm down.
5.  Overall conditioning is important. Don't focus overly much on your arm, or you will inevitably ask too much of it. Your exercise program should enhance overall strength and endurance.
6.  If you ever have pain associated with pitching—no matter how minor it may seem—take it seriously. Talk to your coach or parents and consider seeing a doctor. Also, there are special injuries and problems that can arise from the combination of strenuous sports and still-growing bones, tendons, and muscles. You are putting your baseball career at far more risk by ignoring pain than by having it checked out.

## PITCHER ON DEFENSE

Pitching is a crucial part of baseball. In many ways, it is its centerpiece. But a pitcher must develop the other skills of baseball, since the position has many responsibilities other than the pitching. As pitcher, you are a member of the defensive team and at various times it will fall to you to:

- Field bunts
- Hold runners on base
- Back up plays at home plate
- Cover first base when the first baseman is fielding

### Holding runners on first
What pitchers really need are eyes in the backs of their heads to watch the guy who's taking a lead. Certainly, pitchers have a lot less to worry about when there's no one on base.

   You must know when to try for the pickoff and when not to try. But remember, as we mentioned earlier, any maneuver on the mound that fools a runner into thinking a pitch is coming, when it isn't, is against the rules. You're not allowed to fake a pitch, or balk, as it's called. It can be easy to accidentally balk when a hitter is up and you are trying to pitch *and* pick a runner off base. The umpire is watching you for this type of infraction. If you start to throw to home and direct it to first base instead, that's a balk. Some rules to keep in mind:

1)  The rules say you must throw in the direction you step with your striding foot. (Your striding foot is your left foot if you're right-handed.)  If you step toward it, then make sure to throw toward it, whether it's home or first.

2) You may choose not to throw to second or third even if you do step toward them, whether on or off the rubber. In other words, you are allowed to fake a throw to second or third.

3) Step off the rubber. If you're off the rubber, a balk can't be called and the runner probably won't try to steal.

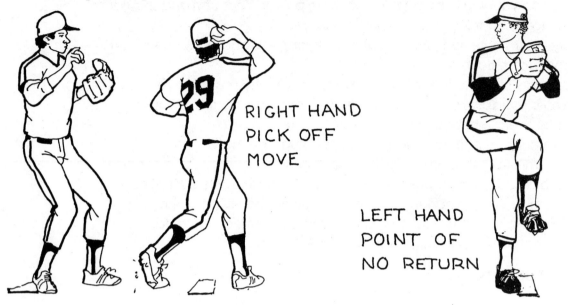

RIGHT HAND
PICK OFF
MOVE

LEFT HAND
POINT OF
NO RETURN

### How to throw the pickoff

*Right-handed pitchers.* You have your back to first base, so you must first turn your head just enough to *clearly* catch sight of the runner out of the corner of your eye. To throw to the base, you are going to literally hop up in the air and spin—and you *must* land with both feet off the rubber. Use a three-quarter overhand throw. Be quick and accurate.

*Left-handed pitchers.* Since your normal pitching stance has you facing toward first, you should never have any trouble holding runners on base. The rules say that left-handed pitchers still must step toward first base when throwing a pickoff. In your stance, when you raise your leg to pitch, it's very similar to beginning to step toward first. If you continue raising and pivoting until your lifted leg crosses back over your standing leg, it's too late to pickoff—you must pitch, or it's a balk. If you intend to pickoff, be careful how far you raise your leg and keep looking toward home as long as you can before turning to throw. Don't telegraph the pickoff.

### Backing up plays

Pitchers should back up plays at home plate, at first when the first baseman is fielding, and at second and third for throws from the outfield.

Defensive players continually back each other up. They are there for each other in case of overthrows, in case of an error, or when a player is pulled out of position. Usually, the backup players position themselves behind the player or base.

A pitcher should back up throws to third base or home plate by being as deep as possible behind them. It's easy to move forward toward the ball and make the play, but not so easy to back up, and a very serious situation if a wild throw passes you altogether.

# Catching

If the position of catcher is the one you want to play, you probably already know what a big job it is. In baseball, the catcher has some of the same kinds of responsibilities that a quarterback does in football. As catcher, you are the only defensive player with a clear view of the whole field and all the players. Also, you must be the most knowledgeable player on the team. The other players will look to you for guidance, and you also must work very closely with the pitcher. No one has to know more about all the aspects of baseball than you.

Along with catching pitches, you must make sure, before each pitch, that the players are in the right places in the field. You must learn and remember as much as you can about the skills of each batter so you can direct the fielders to move back, play shallow, or shift right or left, according to the strength of the batter. You must know your team's tactical objectives and what runners are likely to do in any given situation. You must know the styles and abilities of your own pitchers and know how to communicate with them during the play. On top of that, you have definite fielding responsibilities.

But, before you become proficient at any of this, you must get used to wearing all that gear.

## CATCHER'S GEAR

The first time you suit up for catcher's duty you'll feel buried in gear. The job of catcher can be dangerous, and the gear is there to protect you from being injured. For the gear to succeed in protecting you, you must have the proper items and they should fit well and be in good repair. This will help to ensure not only less pain and injury when you are hit by the ball—and you *will* be hit by the ball—but less general discomfort, more confidence, and therefore a better performance.

### Helmet and face mask
Catchers wear a special kind of helmet called a skullcap, with a face mask designed to be strapped over it and no earflaps. Both skullcap and face mask should fit snugly. They should not have cracks or tears, and the straps and fasteners should be in good shape. Also, make sure you always wear your throat protector.

### Chest protector
Even with a chest protector, a foul tip that hits your torso will smart. Don't worry, the protector softens the blow a good deal; if it doesn't, something is wrong with your gear or you aren't wearing it properly. *It should be snug against your chest.* It shouldn't jiggle and jounce, which can distract you and restrict your movements. Make sure that your chest protector can be fastened securely. If you have the option, choose the kind of protector that has an extension to protect the groin area.

For girls, chest protectors come with inserts to offer greater protection to the breast area. Don't be inclined to discard the extra pads. Situations will arise where you *will* need that extra bit of protection.

### Shin guards

You can't function with shin guards banging around and hiking up your legs. Learn how to strap them on so that they aren't uncomfortably tight, but tight enough to stay in place. The latches should be on the outside of your legs, so the two legs don't latch together. The most common shin guards have four straps, with the "extra" strap holding the guard around the top of the knee, and leather extensions on the sides to protect the softer area of the leg. Make sure to strap your guards on the way the manufacturer intended.

### Catcher's mitt

All players, especially catchers, sometimes hold their index finger out of the glove for relief. It's not recommended to use your throwing hand *behind* the mitt to steady it. You need that hand ready to make a quick throw if runners are on base.

### Cup

No escape, guys. All players, especially catchers, should wear a protective cup.

## CATCHER-PITCHER TEAMWORK

In the game of baseball, catchers and pitchers form a team within a team. The previous chapter touched on the great variety of pitches that might be thrown, most of them pitches that travel quite fast. When you are catching, you need to know what pitch to expect, whether a fastball, curve, change-up, or other type of pitch. If you don't know, there's a good chance you will fail to catch the pitch, and that, of course, can lead to other problems.

Pitchers and catchers communicate over the space between home plate and the mound with hand signals given by the catcher. These are given discreetly, with the catcher sheltering his hand between his legs, as shown in the illustration. You want your signals to be visible only to the pitcher and the middle infielders. When no offensive players are on base who can "eavesdrop" on your signs—a runner on first couldn't see them, but a runner on second could—the universal fingering system can be used. In this system, one finger signals a fastball, two a curve, three a slider, four a change-up, and a fist indicates a pitchout.

Once there's a chance the opponents can see your signals—a runner on second base, for instance—you must use a code system that only your teammates can decipher. Many signaling systems have been used by various catchers over the years. Whatever you and your team decide on, the important thing is to keep it simple. Don't create a system that is so complex that you all get confused. One way is to flash several signals, after agreeing beforehand which one (the second or fourth, for example) is the real signal.

However your team decides to do it, all pitchers and catchers must be up on the system *before game time*, then stick to the system. You can't give instructions about your signaling code every time a pitching switch is made. Shortstops and second basemen also should know the system, to help them anticipate a pitchout and throw so they can tag out the runner taking a lead from second in hopes of advancing to third.

As catcher, the signs you flash to the pitcher may be orders from the manager. Or, they may simply be suggestions. It depends on what your team has decided. Often, you and the pitcher will come to the same conclusion, so the signaling serves to confirm the obvious. However, for whatever reason, the pitcher may not want the pitch you suggest. When he rejects the signal you give him, the pitcher will shake his head from side to side. In this case, you give another signal, and another, until you can agree. But agree quickly, because you can't mess around for too long once a hitter steps up to the plate.

When giving signals, be as close to the batter as you can be without interfering with the batter. This will make it harder for him to glimpse your signal. Also, take a position that allows you to switch to your receiving position as simply as possible. When signaling, your feet should be parallel and twelve or so inches apart. Your back should be straight, head up, elbows close to your body, with your glove hand resting on your leg to help shield the sign.

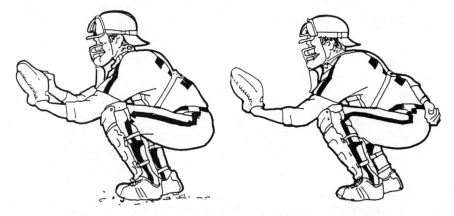

For catching, your position changes distinctly. Once the hitter takes his stance and you and the pitcher have agreed on a pitch, you should shift your weight forward on the balls of your feet and move your hands into catching position. Your feet should be spread out wider than your shoulders, with your right foot (if you're right-handed) slightly back and the heels of both feet only slightly touching the ground.

Many catchers prefer a stance that is neither standing nor squatting—with thighs not quite parallel to the ground, and your backside even with your knees, as if you had lowered yourself into a short chair, but stopped. Your knees are well protected in this position.

As a catcher, the fingers of your throwing hand can get hurt when the batter hits a foul tip. The ball, just barely touched by the bat, changes direction slightly but loses very little of its power. Keep your ungloved hand behind your mitt if there are runners on base, so your bare fingers won't get hurt, but you can still throw quickly. If no one's on base, keep it behind your back.

Some catchers like to kneel on one or two knees, but your legs are less protected this way and it's much more difficult to get up quickly. Other catchers try sitting on their heels, but you are more vulnerable like this, even wearing your cup. The "chair" position takes work. In the beginning, it will tire your legs, but as your muscles develop it will be much easier.

You will have to experiment and find a position that suits you, and one that allows you to perform best. No matter what the fine points of this position are, make sure to stay about an arm's length from the hitter, and no farther. Also, if you or your glove are struck by the hitter, the rules blame *you* and the hitter is awarded first base.

Other pointers:

- Frame the strike zone for the pitcher. Position yourself right behind the plate or shift slightly inside or outside, depending on circumstance. Hold your mitt up for the pitcher to target.
- Keep your eyes open as the hitter swings. Don't turn your head.
- Let the pitch come to you; don't reach for it or go toward it unless you must in order to catch it.
- Between pitches, check the position of the fielders before you give the new signal. Stay aware of the positioning of the fielders. When a long-ball hitter is up, the outfielders should back up. If they're not doing this on their own, you should gesture to them. You also should see that they move in for weaker hitters, and position themselves for left- and right-handed hitters.
- Squat down, kneel on your knees, or straighten up between pitches. This keeps you limber. Keep an eye on the runners on base.

### FRAMING THE PITCH

Catching pitch after hard pitch is one of those things that takes a great deal of skill and yet can look so simple. There are many ingredients in catching pitches effectively.

*Glove angle.* When a pitch is high, you'll naturally hold your glove fingers up. High or low, inside or outside, hold the glove fingers up if at all possible, in order to create something of a visual trick for the umpire's benefit. If you're holding the glove in the way you would for a strike, maybe the umpire can be eased into seeing a strike. For a pitch in the outside corner, funnel the glove from the outside in.

*Balance.* When you are well balanced, planted firmly in a comfortable receiving position, you can sway to make the catch. The point is, don't dance around and swat at the ball. As with any kind of catching, keep yourself in front of the ball.

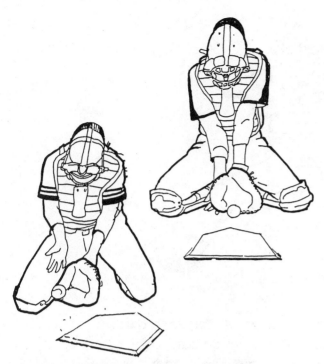

**Getting rid of the mask and turning back on a pop-up**

There's only one time when the catcher has priority over the other fielders catching pop flies, and that's when you or the pitcher might go for it. The first rule, of course, is that whoever can best catch it, should catch it.

If it's yours, you must quickly take off your mask and locate the ball exactly. Grab your mask under your chin and pull it up and out. Throw the mask away from where you think the ball is coming down so you won't trip on it.

Usually, pop flies behind the plate and foul lines are spinning in such a way that they will tend to drift back to the infield. Therefore, you need to put your back to the infield so the dropping ball will drift to you.

To catch a pop, hold your glove up and sight the ball as it falls. Use both hands, pointing your fingers up with the mitt at your shoulders or higher. Sight the ball over the top edge of the mitt fingers. That way you can see it right into the mitt. Remember:

- Remove your mask
- Toss the mask away from the action
- Turn to face the ball

## BLOCKING THE BALL IN THE DIRT

The hardest thing to catch is the low ball in the dirt. Don't scoop it. A fast, breaking pitch will probably skitter away if you try. Your first priority is to block the ball and stop it in front of you. Make yourself into the best wall you can. If the ball's in front of you, drop to your knees and press your arms to your side so your arms, glove, and legs form a wall that blocks the ball. If the ball comes to the side, angle your body wall over to it, dropping your knees to the ground and lowering your shoulder down on the ball side.

In both cases, the point is to position your body so you have the maximum chance of stopping the ball. Keep your arms close to your body and go down with glove and arms to block the ball. Get it into your throwing hand as soon as you can.

## Throwing out runners

It's a long way from second base to home plate. You must be able to throw across that distance, hard and fast. If your opponents know you can't do it, or suspect you can't do it, they'll steal second base every time. The runner's going to beat the ball if you have to throw it high to get it there. So what can you do? Strengthen your arm, and practice. If you can't do it now, make it a priority to get there.

As the pitcher begins every windup, the catcher should glance at the base runners to see if they're moving. Your throwing hand will already be directly behind your glove. When the pitch comes, catch it normally and jump to your feet and into a throwing stance.

## Tagging runners at the plate

The catcher can't block the plate without the ball (the rules forbid interference with the runner). Wait for the throw facing the play, with your left foot on home plate and your right foot to the right of the plate. Catch the throw with two hands and turn and drop onto your right knee, leaving your left shin guard to block the plate. As you lower yourself, bring your free hand into your glove and hold the ball firmly. The runner knows that the ball can be knocked out of the bulky catcher's mitt and will try to do that. So, for safety, make the tag with the back of your glove.

There's no need to beat yourself up. If the throw arrives ahead of the runner, take a few steps down the third-base line and as the runner arrives to bash you, tag his belt buckle and spin away or roll away from the impact. Try to keep on your feet, since after a tag play at the plate, you'll often need to stand up immediately and check for any other runners trying to advance.

# 3. Offense

## At Bat

Just as you can list all the ingredients of a pitch, it is possible to list all the ingredients of batting—stance, grip, the motions. It's up to you to take all these elements and turn yourself into a hitter. You'll find, with practice and concentration, that you can be a capable hitter. Be warned: some players knock themselves out for years, and manage only to become competent. You can tremendously improve your chances of winning the batting title by having a good, fundamentally sound stance and swing.

### SAFETY FIRST

*Helmet.* You should wear a helmet when you bat, and little leaguers also should wear them when they run the bases. You should practice this during batting practice, too. The kind with earflaps on both sides is best. The reason to wear your helmet *all* the time—for practice *and* games—is for safety, but also so that you'll become accustomed to wearing it.

*Drop the bat.* When batting, *drop* the bat, don't fling it. More than one innocent bystander has been injured by the flung bat of a hitter excited about his performance. Also, when limbering up in the on-deck circle, be aware of the other players and don't go swinging when someone is near.

### THE BAT

Hitting that little baseball, traveling at speeds that would get you a ticket on the interstate, with what is little more than a broomstick, may be one of the most difficult things to do in the entire world of sports, so take every advantage you can. Choose a bat that you can swing, not one that swings you.

When choosing a bat, choose the one that's best for you. If you're slightly built, grabbing a mega-bat won't make up for it—it will set you back. To be most effective, smaller players should use lighter bats. A lighter bat is the best way for you to get more hits. What sends the ball is bat speed; so choose a bat that allows you to swing easily, without strain.

Youth-league bats vary from 28 to 33 inches and from 27 to 30 ounces, with high school, college, and pro bats being larger. If someone has given you a bat for a gift or you inherited one from an older sibling, it might not be right for you.

Pick up the heaviest bat you think will suit you, then take it and hold it out with one hand, parallel to the ground. If you can comfortably hold it there steadily for a few seconds, it will probably serve you just fine. If not, choose a slightly lighter one until it passes this test.

Another giveaway that you are using a bat that's too heavy will be the tendency to "choke up" on the bat. If you find yourself gripping it not down near the knob, where you should, but a few inches higher, the bat's too heavy for you. At times, you will deliberately choke up on the bat, for instance, to gain more control when you have two strikes and are protecting the plate. However, the weight of the bat shouldn't be forcing you to choke up.

The bat is designed to be swung from the knob end. If this seems very difficult in the beginning with *any* bat, don't despair. Experiment with bats of varying lengths and thicknesses, and find the one that fits.

Remember which bat you chose, or if there are several, remember the weight stamped on it, and use it as consistently as possible, both for practice and play.

## THE GRIP

Just as when you grip a ball, you should hold a bat with your fingers. It's the fingers that give the control to your grip. As you stand with your side toward the pitcher, your outside hand—the one nearest the pitcher—should be lower on the bat, near the knob. As the illustration shows, place your other hand just above the outside hand. Encircle the bat with the fingers of both hands. Press your fingers together; don't splay them. Don't press the bat against the palm, but hold it with your fingers. Your fingers should come around to meet your thumbs. Hold it firmly, but not so tightly that you tie your entire upper body in knots when you swing. Note in the illustration that the fingers form roughly parallel lines.

Many novice players hold the bat so the knuckles at the base of their fingers on each hand line up. This tends to lock their wrists and makes it impossible for them to get good bat speed. If the batter keeps his or her middle knuckles nearly aligned during the swing, the bat can be whipped quickly through the ball.

## THE STANCE

According to the rules, you *must* keep both feet in the batter's box while you hit. If one foot goes all the way outside the line, you will be called out. The safest approach, and a good position for hitting, is to center yourself in the box. You're less likely to accidentally step out if you put a few inches between your feet and the line. Also, when centered in the box, you're best prepared for whatever kind of pitch comes.

As the illustration shows, a good beginning stance includes:

- *Feet.* Within the box, your feet should be parallel to each other and planted slightly more than shoulder-width apart.
- *Head.* Put your batting helmet on. Step into the batter's box with your side and your face's profile to the pitcher. Turn your head and look over your shoulder. Watch for the pitch with both eyes, holding your chin up. Keep your head and eyes level, not tilted.

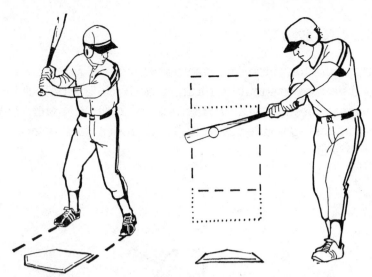

- *Arms.* Coaches used to tell players to raise their elbow back to shoulder height or higher as they prepared to swing. Many of today's coaches believe that batters get better results by keeping their elbows down, and out about six inches from their sides. With your arms like this, raise the bat so that it is more or less perpendicular to the ground.
- *Legs.* Take a position in the batter's box where you can cover the whole plate with the sweet part of the bat. Your front foot should be a little ahead of your shoulder and your back foot running the same direction as the back of the batter's box. Bend your knees with your weight balanced equally between your two feet. Lean forward a bit while making sure your front shoulder is pointed at the pitcher. Bring the bat back about halfway between straight up and horizontal. Concentrate, but keep relaxed and loose.

The stance described above is a common one and a very good way for beginning batters to start forming a personal style in their stance. There are many variations you can try. Players in the minor and major leagues all seem to have their own personal batting stance. If you stick with the game, you'll fine-tune a variation on this basic stance and make it your own.

One common stance variation is in the positioning of the feet. When a right-handed batter stands with his left foot (the one closer to the pitcher) slightly closer to home plate, it's called a *closed stance*; when the right foot is closer to the plate, it's an *open stance*.

It's a good idea to become perfectly at ease with the normal stance before you do a lot of experimenting.

## STRIKE ZONE

When you're in the box, in the basic stance, ready to swing, the strike zone is the space above the plate between your knees and shoulders. Obviously, the strike zone changes slightly depending on the height of the batter, your crouch, and the umpire who's calling the game. And in real life, umpires tend to call the strike zone lower—in fact, they almost universally call it just above the waist to about mid-calf. There's no explanation for this; it's just one of the quirks of the game.

## THE DECISION TO SWING

While you appraise the pitch and decide whether to swing, your body should be coiled and your eyes should remain steadily on the ball. Remain poised for the pitch. Train yourself to wait and watch the ball. You will never hit anything if your swing is a reaction to the pitcher's arm. It should always be a reaction to the ball, which you are watching.

## THE SWING

### Cock
When you prepare for the swing:

- Begin to slightly curl back your shoulder that is nearest the pitcher.
- Cock your hands back very slightly *without raising or lowering them.*
- Pull the bat back.
- Slightly twist your hips, shoulders, and bat back until your body and bat are fully coiled and ready to swing.

### The stride
The stride moves your body from the coil into the swing. Slide your foot forward slightly toward the pitcher. This is a slow, short, and soft step that occurs as a natural consequence of your coiling back and will seem almost simultaneous with it. Shift your weight only slightly to your front foot and press your back foot against the ground. Keep your eyes on the ball. Your hips will begin to rotate toward the pitcher as you begin to swing.

## The swing

Now you have had enough time to judge the pitch and have decided to swing. Throw your hands at the pitch, and if you've done everything described so far, your hands will explode forward with all the power of the stride and turn behind them. Keep your chin down, eyes on the ball.

   Your front arm straightens while your rear elbow stays bent near your body. Transfer your weight onto your front leg as the bat slashes a downward angle through the strike zone. Make a downward diagonal swing. Don't arc down and loop back up. If you hit the top half of the ball, you may have yourself a line drive or at least a good grounder.

## Follow-through

Your weight should go almost entirely onto your front foot, while your rear foot pivots and the heel comes up. Your head should remain still and down, both eyes focused on the point of contact.

   As your follow-through continues, your head should turn toward the field as your wrists turn over to allow the bat to complete its arc. During follow-through, your rear foot should neither lift nor drag, and keep your balance throughout the follow-through.

## BUNTING

First of all, keep in mind that your goal when bunting will probably be simply to advance the runner who's on base. *You* will *probably* be out. As a matter of strategy, you sacrifice an out for the success of the team. However, you should run hard, forcing the defense to execute perfectly—it will improve your teammate's chances of advancing and, you never know, a mistake by the defense could mean that your sacrifice bunt gets you to first base.

If your league allows bunting (some youth leagues don't), you should take the time to practice it. There's more than one way to bunt, but doing any kind of bunting well takes practice.

One way of bunting is to step around and squarely face the pitcher. The other method is to pivot on the balls of your feet and turn your hips and shoulders to the pitcher. Either way, remember to keep both feet inside the batter's box and get into your bunting stance soon enough so that you are balanced and have a steady hold on the bat for the hit. Also remember that the point of bunting, especially in the beginning, is to contact the ball, period. When you first try bunting, concentrate on just dropping the ball, not where it drops. Finally, bunt only good pitches! If the pitcher's going to walk you, let him.

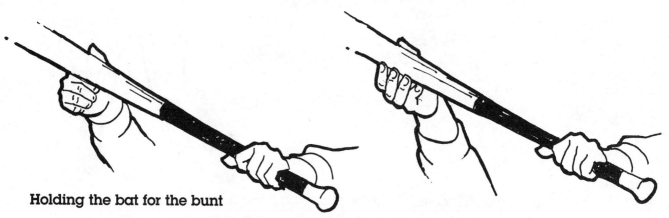

**Holding the bat for the bunt**

Whichever position you take for the bunt, the way you handle the bat will be the same.

1. Keep your bottom hand near the bat's knob and slide your top hand up the barrel, holding it between your thumb and index finger. Keep your other fingers bent behind the bat.
2. Hold the bat at a 45-degree angle, and start with it held toward the top of the strike zone.
3. To come down for a low strike, bend your knees rather than your hips. Don't raise your bat out of the strike zone to bunt a high pitch.
4. Wait for the pitch to come to you, and push the bat forward softly, to stop—not propel—the ball. Imagine yourself as trying to catch the ball with the bat.
5. Hold the bat over and in front of the plate.
6. Holding the bat's knob lower than the tip of the barrel can make hitting a pop fly less likely.

TARGET AREAS
FOR BUNTING

## Pivoting

This is probably the simplest, safest way to bunt. Instead of turning completely around to face the pitcher square-on, pivot at the hips. By doing so, you can basically stand and look at the ball in the usual way—the way you feel most at ease. It also hides your intention longer than does the square-on method. Start in your normal batting stance. When the pitcher begins the throwing motion, bend at the knees, extend your arms, and face the pitcher with your upper body.

## Square-on

This is the classic bunting method. You start in the basic batting stance. When the pitcher winds up, turn your body and fully face him. Pull your back foot up to the level of your front foot. Your feet should be spread at least shoulder-width apart, but farther apart is better, with the weight on the balls of your feet.

# Baserunning

## RUNNING

You're not a klutz, but do you *know* how to run? There are ways you can improve your form. Running form is something worth spending time on, since when the manager looks at his new talent at the start of the season, one of the first things he'll ask the group to do is run a few sprints. The coach can tell, just by looking at running form, who are the natural athletes and who may not be starting material.

When running on the base path, *lean forward*. Pull your arms and hands in toward your body and pump them in sync, left arm moving with right leg. Also, hold your feet straight, not pointing in or out. Run on the balls of your feet and toes, not on your heels. Take medium-size strides. You won't run your fastest by trying to take huge strides and grab the most territory you can with every step. You can't effectively use all the muscles of your legs, both thigh *and* calf, that way. The only time to take very rapid small strides is if you expect you may need to change direction quickly—for instance, if you are caught in a rundown.

Work for speed. Get a stopwatch and race yourself in thirty-yard dashes. As you practice and play more, you will naturally get stronger and faster, but some of us are innately good runners and simply faster than others. Anyway, if you realize you really need more speed rounding the diamond, congratulations! You're getting some hits!

As a general rule, if you are a runner on base, you must run when you are signaled by the third-base coach, or you are forced to run because of the play in progress. You should always run hard, taking good hard turns *expecting* to advance from first to third or from second to home.

The important points you should remember about baserunning are: watch the ball, run *fast*, know when to go for more than one base, *when* to look to the third-base coach for information, and how to run the base paths, tag, and turn the bases correctly.

### Being ready

For base runners already on base, being prepared to GO is a good way to win a few extra seconds. With the batter up, you should be poised low, on your toes, your weight low but balanced, and all your attention on the strike zone.

### Lead

When on base, you can get a little bit of a head start by "leading" from the base. This means that you don't stand touching the bag, but move a few feet off your base in the direction of the next base, in order to make your job easier and put pressure on the defense.

With a lead, you won't have quite as far to run, which makes it easier to steal a base and a double play harder for the defense to pull off. Also, leading off the base makes the pitcher have to pay you a little more attention, and may actually distract him or her. If you cause the pitcher to throw a ball instead of a strike, to balk, or throw a wild pitch—good! When you take your lead, sidestep off your base. Hold there in a very slight crouch—knees bent a little, arms too, hands in front of your body. Stay balanced and steady on your feet and ready to run, either back to the base or on to the next one.

Be ready to move quickly, because the pitcher will try to pick you off. You should lead only out to where you can safely get back when the pitcher tries to pick you off. This, of course, depends on how quick and how alert you are, but is generally your body length plus one step—as much distance as you can dive back in one motion.

*Note*: In official Little League play, players are *not* allowed to lead off the bases.

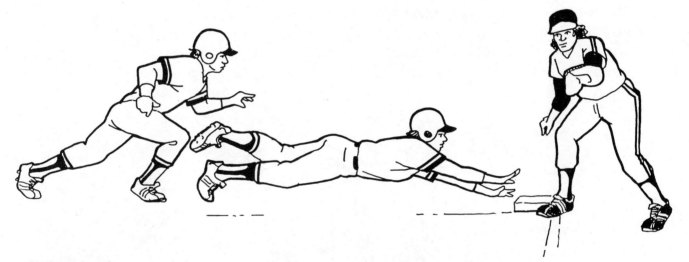

**Getting back**

When the pitcher does throw to your base, get back to the base fast! You can dive headfirst.

You don't have nearly the speed up that you do when baserunning and sliding, so you should be a lot less likely to get hurt in a headfirst dive back to the base. When you do this, aim for the edge of the bag; that gives the baseman just that much more space to reach before tagging you. Also, dive in a way that protects you. Dive down and across in a straight line from your crouched, ready-to-run position. Don't throw yourself high to arc down—your fall will be much harder, *and* will take longer. Hold your arms out wider than your shoulders, break your fall with your hands, and turn your head away so you won't get tagged in the face or hit by the ball. Include this headfirst dive in your practice routine.

## WATCHING THE BALL

When the ball has been hit, you as a runner need to "watch" the ball. Of course, there's also plenty else you have to do, like running, tagging bases, avoiding fielders, and watching the third-base coach. Watching the ball doesn't mean standing there with your hands at your sides, gaping at the ball. You must learn to integrate watching the ball, keeping your eye on other things, and moving.

Your first priority as a base runner is to run, *quickly*, to the next base. However, it *is* helpful for you to know, as you run, what kind of hit you're running on (a pop-up, a grounder, or whatever) and where it's headed. For example, if a fly ball is caught, you must return to the base and tag up before trying for the next base. You are not forced to run. If two outfielders collide and the ball reaches the fence, then you try for extra bases.

You need to decide how many bases you will possibly be able to take, whether and when to start your curve for extra bases, if you are going to have to slide, and so on. To make these split-second decisions, you must keep your eye on the ball in some fashion, and on the first- and third-base coaches.

No player starts out being able to run, tag bases, and watch the ball. They learn to *locate* the ball and continue to glance or peek at it as they go.

Making good running judgments is one of those things that come up to speed only with experience, which means practice, practice, practice.

Remember, as we said in the Introduction, cleats are your best bet for baseball. You will get a lot better speed running the bases in cleats.

## GETTING OUT OF THE BATTER'S BOX

You've hit the ball and put it in play! You're not the batter now, you're a base runner. Drop the bat, don't fling it. Leave the batter's box as soon as you've hit the ball. If you batted from the right, push off hard with your right foot (left foot if you're left-handed). From the very first step, direct yourself to first. Take a couple of short, choppy strides and stay low while working up speed and getting into the long, full strides you'll need to take you there.

Don't stop to watch the ball. Standing and watching to see what kind of hit you got could get you tagged out rather than safe on base. You must know whether to run straight to first or curve out and try for second, and so you'll have to work out a method of locating and sizing up the ball and running at the same time. Commonly, runners on their way to first base look briefly to their left once they get going fast. If the ball is being fielded and you must beat it to first, keep running at top speed straight through the base—that's faster than leaping, sliding, or any other desperation move. Slide to avoid a tag, but not a throw.

Remember, run *through* the bag and not *to* it. This will help you keep up speed. Slowing down for the bag can doom you to an out. The rules allow you to run far beyond first base and still be safe. But be careful—don't turn even slightly toward a second base in a way that might look like an attempt, or you could be tagged out.

## HOW MANY BASES?

Judging when and how far to run is nearly as important as being able to hit. Here are a few general outlines:

When a ground ball doesn't make it out of the infield, getting to first base will depend on two things: the speed and competence of the fielders, and the speed of the runner. This is a race against time, and you must move as fast as you can to beat the throw to first and put pressure on the fielders that might cause them to make an error.

A ground ball into the outfield will probably get you to first.

A ground ball that seems to be going past the outfielders and deep into the outfield will give you a good chance to try for a second base.

A fly ball will get the hitter to first *if it isn't caught*. And, if it *isn't* caught, making it to second is a distinct possibility. Remember, never get the first or third out of an inning at third base. Getting the first out might blow a big inning for your team, and getting the third out will end the inning when the next batter up might have driven you in for a score.

### Turn at first—trying for second base

Great! A nice strong hit to the outfield—you can make it to second base. Now you shouldn't run *through* first. As you head there, you must get yourself turned toward second base. Head for first, but then, as the diagram shows, arc out into foul territory well before you arrive. Near first, begin your turn by pushing hard with your right foot and leaning left. Arc about twelve feet out into foul territory—anything less will probably make you slow down too much to make the turn. Hit the inside of the base with either foot.

Turning, curving, or "bellying" around the bases also applies when you're going from first to third, or second to home.

## SLIDING

You may be one of those players who love to slide, to practice slides, and who, during games, will never take the base upright if there's any way to justify sliding. Get a grip! Sliding is *not* done for dramatic effect—it is an emergency means of avoiding a tag—maybe! When getting from base to base, speed is your first priority. Sliding doesn't speed you up, it slows you down. Use it only when it's the most likely way to arrive safely.

Now, as for sliding quickly, a head-first dive will get you there the fastest, but head-first diving from a full run is very dangerous and can result in sprained wrists, bloody noses, and worse. Don't do it unless your coach has taught you the slide very carefully, and if you do use it, keep your batting gloves on all the way around the base paths.

The safest way to slide, as illustrated here, is to make a controlled fall, *feet first*, with your weight coming down mostly on your backside and lower back and one foot bent behind the knee. You should begin falling backward first. You won't be quite horizontal as you slide into the base feet first. If you instinctively tuck one leg up—good. That tuck, as shown in the illustration, is an important part of a safe slide. If you don't do it automatically, train yourself to do it. If you slide deliberately and don't tense up, you'll be less likely to get hurt. Keep your head and shoulders up enough so you can watch for collisions and avoid the tagger. And make sure you hit the base—why go through all that trouble and then miss it?

The key element is *control*. If you begin to lower your body about ten feet from the base, the momentum of the run will propel you across the base. Once you are down and going toward the base, focus on good form and control, both to protect yourself and so that you will be able to pop back up immediately after the slide. You never know what sort of a wild throw you may have forced, and you want to be ready to take advantage of the opportunity to grab the next base.

### Avoidance slide

The ball has beat you to the base and you are in danger of being tagged out. This is the time for a maneuver called a *hook slide*. You will try to hook the bag with your foot while bending your body away from the tag.

On your approach to the base, begin a normal slide, but stretch your foot to the bag and at the same time roll your upper body away from the tag. Hook the bag with the foot on your straight leg, which is your stronger side, while allowing your body's momentum to carry the rest of you to the side and away from danger.

### STEALING BASES

Sliding goes hand in hand with stealing bases, something we all love to try to accomplish.

Stealing is risky, and you won't endear yourself to your teammates if you're always trying and failing. Stealing is best saved for situations where you've little chance of advancing otherwise. For example, if you're a runner on first, there's one out, and the bottom of the order is coming up, then you might think about stealing.

Here are the necessary first steps for a successful steal:

1. Have the longest lead that's safe. Don't put yourself so far away from the base that you can't get back.
2. Watch the pitcher.
   *Know when to steal.* The pitcher is not allowed to fake a pitch to home. Pitchers will try to hide their intentions as long as possible. They don't want you, the runner, to know early that they are committed to the throw to home. You want to know as early as you can, because it will help you steal. Figuring out the pitcher's moves is an important part of stealing.
3. Begin your steal as the pitcher begins to stride.
4. Start with a hard push into a crossover step.
5. *Run!*
6. Slide!

Once the decision has been made to steal, most right-handed players will start with a crossover step while pushing off hard on their right foot. Throw your body forward. This first move should be explosive. It takes an explosion to go from a standstill to a fast run. Keep your weight low and tilt your upper body toward the base.

## THE THIRD-BASE COACH

To keep an eye on the ball, base runners rounding second or third base need eyes in the back of the head. The third-base coach's job is to be those extra eyes.

When the ball is hit, the third-base coach moves to where advancing runners can see him. For example, if the ball is hit to right field, this means the third-base coach might move out toward left field and circle his arm to tell a runner from first to round second and try for third. If the runner is rounding third, the coach might move up the line toward home.

When taking a lead from second, a runner must watch the second baseman. The third-base coach helps by keeping track of the shortstop and any pickoff action that seems to be developing. Usually the coach shouts "okay" if there's no present danger. That okay indicates to the runner that he may take one or two more lead steps; "Okay" again means he can take another step. It's obvious what's meant when the coach shouts "stay" or "back." The third-base coach shouting "go" and circling or windmilling his arm means the runner can take off for the next base.

Windmilling arms mean run; squatting might mean slide; two hands held up could mean "stop at this base." The main thing is to have a system of clear signals that can be recognized quickly and easily by a base runner who can only glance over toward the coach while running at top speed.

# 4. TIPS AND TACTICS

## KNOWING YOUR RESPONSIBILITIES ON DEFENSE

Each position has a particular set of responsibilities. Whatever your position is, you must know your responsibilities. It's also important for you to know what all the other players in the field are expected to do.

Remember, even when you have specialized somewhat in a position, don't limit your options when you're young. To learn baseball well, learn as much as you can about all the positions.

The first responsibility of every player is to understand the game situation and get mentally ready, between pitches, to do what is required. All players should review in their minds the count against the batter, the number of outs, the situation on the base paths, and the score, then glance at the catcher and manager for signals. Players should be mentally prepared by reviewing what the most likely plays will be and reviewing what they will do when these things happen.

As the pitcher winds up, the players should always assume their ready positions and be focused on the play. On every pitch, every fielder should think, "The ball will come to me."

## THE FIRST BASEMAN

The first baseman should field all batted balls from halfway between home and first, and to halfway between first and second. Remember also that fielding all balls thrown to you is a primary responsibility and it is your secondary responsibility to stop runners from getting safely to first base. But stop the runner before he or she ever gets to first and you are all spared a great deal of work down the line.

Normally when you play first base, you stand a few feet in the direction of second, a bit behind the base line. Here, you are best able to:

1.  Field balls in your area.
Often, you must leave the immediate vicinity of the base to field in your area. If you get too far from first base to be able to step on the bag or tag the runner, your second baseman or the pitcher is supposed to cover the base for you. You will probably be close enough to deliver it to that player with an underhand toss.

2.  Catch balls and tag first base.
On a force-out, you must catch the ball thrown to you and touch the base with any part of your body before the runner arrives. The classic technique, when the throw comes right to you, is to stretch out for the catch,

while keeping your back foot on the edge of the base.

Make sure you really know where the ball is headed, though, before you reach for it. It's tricky to shift your weight when you are already off balance.

3.   Hold runners on first.

Stand with your right foot touching the home-plate side of first base. Hold your glove out, toward the pitcher, making a target for the pitcher, and be ready for a throw. Sweep your glove over and down to tag a runner. If the ball is pitched, quickly move away from the base into a normal fielding position.

Your other responsibilities are:

- Throw to second for a double play
- On extra-base hits, back up second and home
- Relay throws from right and center field, or cut off the runners' advance

## THE SECOND BASEMAN

Your fielding responsibilities cover a large area, stretching from the midpoint between first and second, over to second, to behind the pitcher's area to the edge of right and center field. You are right in the midst of the single area where the most action is concentrated.

It's your job to:

- Field balls in your area
- Toss to the shortstop on second and throw to first for force-outs
- Tag out runners between first and second and tag second on force-outs
- Back up first base
- Back up the shortstop
- Relay throws from the outfield

## THE SHORTSTOP

In this position, you are responsible for a large area of the field. This area stretches from second nearly to third and into the outfield. A good place for you to take your stance is in the near outfield between second and third. Part of where you stand will depend on how far you can throw, because you will very often need to make a throw all the way to first base. It's up to you to field all balls in the area. You and the third baseman will stay busy. Most hitters are right-handed, and most of the batted balls will come to the two of you.

It's also your job to:

- Field balls in your area
- Toss to second and throw to first on force-outs
- Relay/cut off throws from the outfield
- Back up second


## THE THIRD BASEMAN

This area doesn't seem large, but it's a long throw to first base and you'll need a good arm. All those right-handed hitters are sending balls your way. Late in the day if the score is close you should guard the third-base line! A good spot for you is a few steps inside the foul line and even with the bag. If you let the ball escape and roll past third, it'll roll and roll and the hitter will probably roll on to second base. In addition to guarding the base line in the late innings of a close game, you must:

- Make the plays at your base
- Throw force-outs to first
- Relay throws from outfield to home and left field
- Back up the shortstop


## OUTFIELDERS

The three outfielders cover more total area than the six infielders cover. Any ball that gets out to them could mean extra bases or runs for your opponent. They also must back up the players on the infield.

### Positions and stance
Outfielders don't bend their knees or lower their bodies as much as infielders, because they might have to straighten and sprint. They hold themselves straighter and not as low down to the ground.

The outfielders should position themselves so that they each can see all of the infield, including the pitcher and catcher. When you play outfield, you will find that you need to adjust your position slightly to avoid having your view blocked by a teammate.

How far out you stand will depend on what's going on in the game: who's hitting, and so on. A good catcher will direct you in for a weaker hitter, out for a stronger one. Another factor is the game situation (how many runners on base, how many outs, for example), and whether the hitter is right-handed (they tend to hit to left field) or left-handed (they tend to hit to right field). Who is pitching and catching can also affect the placement of the outfielders.

**Pop flies**

- Keep the ball in front of you. It's easier to run toward the ball than back for it.
- Judging the ball:
  1) *The wind.* It will take the ball in the direction it is blowing. Move out if the wind is blowing toward you, in if it blows in the direction of home, and left or right accordingly.
  2) *The sun.* Shade your eyes from the sun with your glove, and keep watching the ball.

**Grounders**
Remember, block that ball at all costs. For a grounder to the outfield, bend on your glove-side knee and hold your glove in front of and in between your legs. You want to scoop the ball quickly, but the safest bet is to make sure you present the greatest surface area to stop the ball.

**Communication**
When you are sure that the ball is yours, shout "mine" or "I got it." Don't leave the ball up for grabs. Be brief. Shout your message clearly in one or two words. After a catch is made, shout "relay!" or "home" or whatever you need to say as succinctly as possible.

**Getting the ball in**
Remember to throw in relay. Throw the ball to the farthest teammate you can quickly and accurately reach. When you have a long distance to cover with the ball, one high arcing throw attempted from the outfield to home (or anywhere) will be slower and less accurate than a relay by a couple of fast, straight throws between players.

**Backup**
Many times, the outfielder nearest you will depend on you for backup. Also, infielders might rely on you, depending on the play:

- In right field, you will back up the second baseman. You also will back up plays at first. Be there to catch a ball that gets past first or second.
- Over in left field, you will be called on to back up plays behind third, or back up the shortstop.
- Center fielders will back up plays behind second or the shortstop.

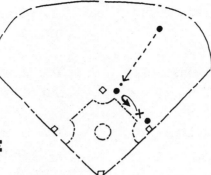

## SOME GOLDEN RULES OF DEFENSE

### Don't let runners advance

The first line of defense is the pitcher. Obviously, if no one gets on base, no one scores. But players do get on base. When they do, the first priority of the defense is to hold the runner on base; don't give them an opportunity to try to advance, whether they're forced to or not.

### Throw in front of the runner or to a central position

When there is no possibility of throwing a runner out, then throw *ahead* of him to the next base. In this way, the first rule of defense is served by not letting a runner advance.

When it's not possible to throw in front of the runner, throw to the most central cutoff player. If you were in right field, with a runner just arriving at third, the pitcher would be the central player that stops the runner from continuing to home.

### Get the sure out

A bird in the hand is worth two in the bush. If you have an out, a *sure out*, always go for it. Don't make a long, difficult throw to home in hopes of preventing a score if your only throw has a slim chance of succeeding and you could easily put the batter out at second. Obviously, this is not a "rule" you should always follow in the ninth inning of a close game.

### Always try for the second (or third) out

After you've gone for the sure out, try for more. That first out may be a caught ball. So, outfielders, always be on the alert after catching a pop fly for the possibility of catching an unaware runner between the bases or a speedster who thinks he can beat your throw. Second basemen, do your job carefully and get the lead runner, then throw to first base.

## FORCE-OUTS

A force-out occurs when a runner is forced to advance. As the player runs, the defensive player at the next base catches the ball and touches base before the runner reaches it.

Generally, the first, second, and third basemen and the shortstop are responsible for force-outs at their respective bases, and the catcher at home. However, if these players are pulled away from the base to field the ball, someone else must cover the force-out at the base:

| | |
|---|---|
| When first baseman fields the ball | The pitcher or second baseman makes the force-out at first |
| When second baseman fields the ball | The shortstop makes the force-out at second |
| When shortstop fields the ball | The second baseman makes the force-out at second |
| When the catcher fields the ball | The pitcher makes the force-out at home |

It is very important for you to know these assignments, because you want to prevent a situation where there is confusion about who is covering the play.

## BUNTS

Fielding softly hit bunts is not easy. These balls don't roll far, so the batter has more time to run while an infielder moves to field the ball, possibly leaving a base uncovered. Again, you don't want everyone on the team trying to field every bunt.

Your team should decide ahead of time who covers what bunt and when. Usually, first and third basemen come forward for bunts on either side; this leaves the remaining three infielders to cover the bases, guarding against the possibility that the hitter will slash one past all three bases.

If there is a runner on second and the ball is bunted down the third-base line, the shortstop covers third to keep that runner from advancing. The pitcher, third baseman, and catcher field bunts closer to their immediate areas. This is a situation where they do not want to butt heads while reaching for the ball. Remember to call out "mine" and to heed your teammate and let him have the ball when he clearly calls for it.

A special danger is a bunt that rolls along right near the foul line. You want to allow it to go foul if that's what it appears it will do. But if you're not sure, and you can field it and get a sure out, *don't wait*—do it.

## PREVENTING STEALS

Stealing is when a runner on base tries to advance when the ball hasn't been hit or a batter walked. Stealing runners are not forced, so the runner must be tagged out. Second base is the one most commonly stolen, in part because the catcher handles the ball a great deal and it's a long way to throw to second from home. If the catcher throws poorly, that runner will succeed in stealing the base. Also, it's hard for a right-handed pitcher to pitch and keep an eye on first base. Some helpful points for stopping a steal:

- Hold the runner as close to the base as possible with pickoff throws.
- The shortstop and second baseman should practice a system of deception concerning who's covering second, so a runner on second will not know if a big lead can be safely taken.
- Pitchouts to the catcher can be tried to more easily catch runners attempting to steal.


- Catchers should not throw when they doubt they can catch the runner. A poor throw could create further opportunities for the runners to advance.
- Always keep your back-up duties in mind:
    If you're the shortstop, you back up second.
    Outfielders, move in, cover for infielders.
    Pitcher, be ready where you are needed.
- Remember, after you've caught the ball, sweep your glove into the runner's path and force him to tag himself out by sliding into it. Lift the glove back up immediately and look for further action.

Pitchers should make sure to communicate to the would-be stealer that you are watching him by looking, by body language, or whatever other means you can while still staying within the rules. And don't forget: *watch him.*

## RELAY TECHNIQUES

The relay man should keep running toward the outfielder who is fielding the ball until the outfielder picks it up. The closer the better. While running, the relay shouts "Relay!" or "Cutoff!" and raises his arms high over his head to get the outfielder's attention even before he looks up, and to give him a clear target when he does. The relay turns his glove side to the outfielder, so when the relay catches the ball he is already poised to quickly throw the ball and beat the runner home.

If the throw is to be cut off, the cutoff man should stand fifty feet from home plate, directly between the catcher and the outfielder with the ball. He should shout and wave just as a relay would. The outfielder aims for his chest, and the cutoff may either turn toward the play on base and catch the ball, or make the play. On the catcher's shouted signal, let the ball bounce once and continue on to the catcher for the play at the plate.

## PITCHING IN THE REAL WORLD

A lot of instruction has been given, here and on practice fields all over the country, about how pitchers should use their fingers, palms, wrists, arms, backs, legs, etc. We can hope that all that instruction at least begins to get you ready to step out on the mound and blank those hitters. Other than the physical ingredients of pitching, you'll find that there's a lot to be learned about when to pitch what and to whom. Here are just a few of the most common pointers beginning pitchers should learn.

Some suggestions for what to do when there's . . .

- . . . no one on base.

You don't have to worry about steals, holding runners on base, or the runner in scoring position (on second or third) who might use a hit as an opportunity to score. All you have to worry about is throwing strikes. If you have a good fastball, use it. And unless those batters tell you, by hitting it, that it's not enough, keep using it.

- . . . a runner on first and one or no outs.

In this situation, many pitchers will keep their pitches low, hoping that the batter hits a grounder that the defense can turn into a double play. Any downward moving curve or low fastball will be harder for a hitter to get up into the air.

- . . . a runner on second or third with one or no outs.

You really want to prevent that score. If you let the batter hit the ball deep enough to the outfield, that guy on third base is in. You need a strikeout or a grounder to get the batter out. If you think the batter will bunt, then pitch high fastballs. Or maybe the batter will pop it up. One way to find out if a bunt is in the offing is to try a pitchout and see if the batter tips you off. Also, maybe your catcher will be able to pick off an overanxious runner.

- . . . a runner on second and you think the batter wants to hit the ball to the right of the infield to get that runner to third.

For a right-handed batter, try to pitch in and high; for a left-hander, out and down. Placing the ball like this encourages any hit ball to go left—toward third—which will make it easier to stop that base runner from advancing.

- . . . a runner on second base.

Many pitchers say it's better in this situation to walk batters than hand them up anything they can hit. The reasoning is that with the batter safely walked, next time the defense may be able to turn a double play or at least a force-out. So, since it won't be any tragedy if you end up walking the batter, this is a good time to try your trickiest pitches. If they work, you'll probably put the batter out. If they don't work, but stray from the strike zone and end up called balls, you walk the batter and there's little harm done.

■ . . . your team's way ahead.

You step in to pitch and your side is already ahead by four runs or more. Unlike the situation described just above, this is no time to attempt your trick pitches, since they are the ones that most often miss. This means that if your side has a healthy lead, *don't* walk 'em—not deliberately and not if you can help it. When your opponents are behind, they need a big inning to catch up; big innings aren't usually made from one great hit after another. Usually they come from hits interspersed with walks, until the bases are loaded and, *wham*—a home run. There goes your lead.

## TIPS FOR THE BATTER

Ted Williams had a long and successful hitting career with the Boston Red Sox. He came away with three "Rules to Hit By":

1.  Get a good pitch to hit.
2.  Pay attention.
3.  Be quick with the bat.

*Getting a good hit.* Concentrate on not swinging at balls outside the strike zone. If you can teach yourself to wait and watch the ball, and not swing at bad balls, you're far more likely to hit the ball when you swing, and when you do hit it, have a much harder, more useful hit.

*Thinking right.* With any kind of organized play, you get to know the strengths of the opposing pitchers. And if you are aware of what they have been known to do on the mound, your guess about what's coming at you is a more educated guess. The pros with the most serious hitting ambition make a lifelong study of pitchers. In general, batters need to psych themselves up. Be enthusiastic, aggressive, eager. Try not to approach the plate with a lump of apprehension in your stomach.

*Swing a quick bat.* Good hits aren't a result of how heavy or strong you are, although that helps. They come from bat speed. Grip the bat properly, so your wrists remain flexible. Step into the pitch and swing like you mean it. Tense muscles will only slow your bat down.

Another tip: think line drive. Imagine sending the ball right back where it came from, down the middle of the field at head height. Make hitting ground balls your priority. Sure, once in a blue moon a ball comes along with "outta the park" written on it. But if a high flyer *doesn't* go out, you're just one clean catch away from an out. On the other hand, a good hard line drive forces the players in the field to catch, throw, and catch—and you may be on base before they can do all that.

## TIPS FOR THE BASE RUNNER

You've made it to first! Now you can relax—oh, no you don't! Your work is cut out for you.

In Part Three, we gave some tips on posture, tagging up, watching the ball, and so on while you run. The following tactical tips will also help you.

Always run and don't hesitate . . .

- . . . on any kind of hit when your team has two outs. Run when you hear the ball crack on the bat. Maybe the sun was in his eyes and the outfielder dropped that "sure" out—and if he did and you didn't hustle, ouch. Your side needs your score. Don't just stand there.
- . . . on a ground ball when you're forced. Don't give the defense an easy out when you can make it close, force an error, distract the defense from another runner—and maybe even make it to the nearest base.
- If you are going to be tagged out, try to get into a rundown. It may distract the defense from another base runner who can advance.

Always . . .

- . . . move a few steps away from the base on every pitch. If it's hit, you have a head start. If it's a wild pitch, you have a head start toward the next base. Watch the ball or the third-base coach and go back and tag if necessary.
- . . . run! Be quick. Even when you get a walk to first, run. They may not be paying any attention to you, and you may be able to cruise right on to second.
- . . . take a base standing if you can, but if you're not sure, slide. Even if it's a sure out, you might unsettle the infielder and cause an error.
- . . . if you've hit a sacrifice bunt down the first base line, and the first baseman decides to try to tag you out, slide into first. Why just run into a tag?

Think steal when . . .

- . . .you're on first, there's one or no outs, and there's a runner on third.
- . . .you're on first, the bottom of the order is up, and your opponents need a double play to end a big inning.

And think run when . . .

- . . .you are on third, and the ball gets by the catcher and the pitcher neglects to cover home.

# Conclusion

For the baseball novice, the material we've presented here may represent a lot of new information. It's up to you to develop the skill and strength. No matter what your age or natural physical ability, if you're mentally and physically prepared to perform the many skills and techniques of the game, you can have a great time practicing and playing.

Someday when you're a veteran player, these elementary techniques for throwing, catching, hitting, and running will be second nature for you. For now, you can take our tips and become better prepared for the challenges and rewards of this popular team sport, and ready to practice hard and play to win.

Remember, baseball players are made, not born.

Books in the *Sports Rules in Pictures* and *Sports Techniques in Pictures* series are available at your local bookstore or wherever books are sold, or for your convenience, we'll send them directly to you. Just call 1-800-631-8571 or fill out the coupon below and send it to:

**The Putnam Publishing Group**
**390 Murray Hill Parkway, Dept. B**
**East Rutherford, NJ 07073**

|  |  |  | US | CANADA |
|---|---|---|---|---|
| _____ | Baseball Rules in Pictures | 399-51597-6 | $7.95 | $10.50 |
| _____ | Baseball Techniques in Pictures | 399-51798-7 | $8.95 | $11.75 |
| _____ | Basketball Rules in Pictures | 399-51590-9 | $7.95 | $10.50 |
| _____ | Football Rules in Pictures | 399-51689-1 | $7.95 | $10.50 |
| _____ | Football Techniques in Pictures | 399-51769-3 | $7.95 | $10.50 |
| _____ | Golf Rules in Pictures | 399-51799-5 | $7.95 | $10.50 |
| _____ | Golf Techniques in Pictures | 399-51664-6 | $7.95 | $10.50 |
| _____ | Hockey Rules in Pictures | 399-51772-3 | $7.95 | $10.50 |
| _____ | Official Little League Baseball® Rules in Pictures | 399-51531-3 | $7.95 | $10.50 |
| _____ | Soccer Rules in Pictures | 399-51647-6 | $7.95 | $10.50 |
| _____ | Soccer Techniques in Pictures | 399-51701-4 | $7.95 | $10.50 |
| _____ | Softball Rules in Pictures | 399-51728-6 | $7.95 | $10.50 |
| _____ | Tennis Rules and Techniques in Pictures | 399-51674-3 | $7.95 | $10.50 |
| _____ | Volleyball Rules in Pictures | 399-51537-2 | $7.95 | $10.50 |

|  |  |
|---|---|
| Subtotal | $_____ |
| Postage & handling* | $_____ |
| Sales tax (CA, NJ, NY, PA, Canada) | $_____ |
| Total amount due | $_____ |

Payable in U.S. funds (no cash orders accepted). $15.00 minimum for credit card orders
*Postage & handling: $2.50 for 1 book, 75¢ for each additional book up to a maximum of $6.25.

Please send me the titles checked above. Enclosed is my:

❏ check        ❏ money order

Please charge my:

❏ Visa        ❏ MasterCard        ❏ American Express

Card #_____ Expiration date _____

Signature as on charge card_____

Name _____

Address _____

City_____ State _____ Zip _____

Please allow six weeks for delivery. Prices subject to change without notice.

Source key #15